FIRST BORN MIDDLE CHILD

MANY MAMAS

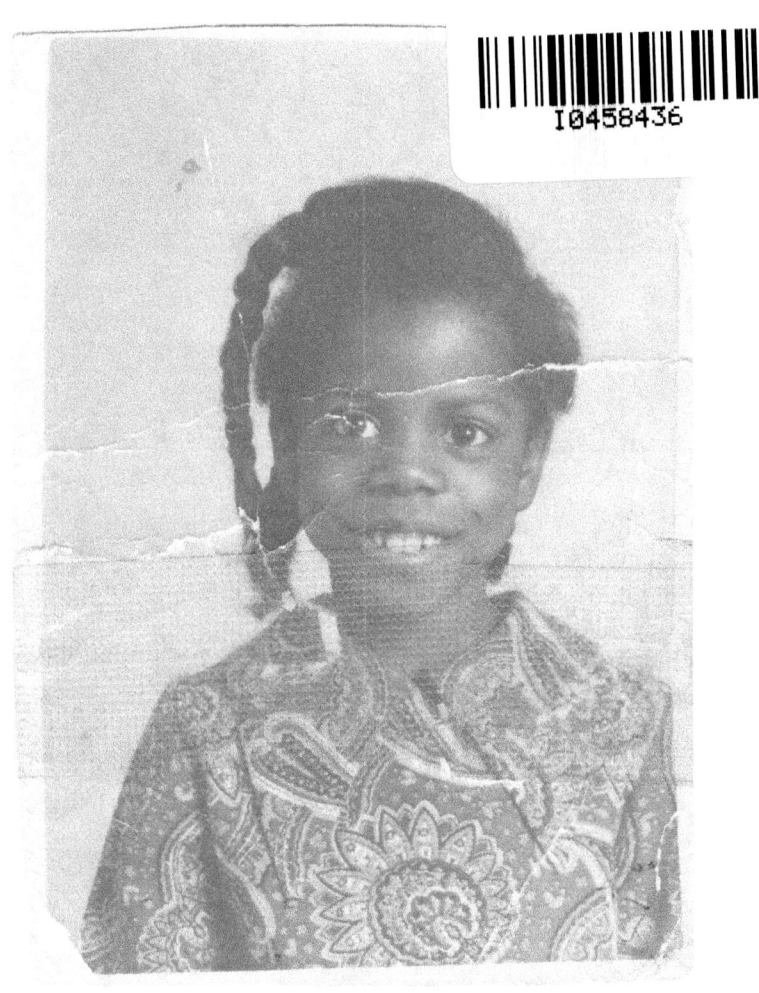

REGINA M. MOORE

Chapbook Press

Schuler Books
2660 28th Street SE
Grand Rapids, MI 49512
(616) 942-7330
www.schulerbooks.com

First Born Middle Child

ISBN 13: 9781957169880

Library of Congress Control Number: 2024911401

Printed in the United States.

BOOK DEDICATION

To my sister and brother

I realized in writing this book, how much more I loved you both. You were my life until you were adults yourselves. I am so glad despite our separate ways sometimes over the years, we are so close now. As I have told you we all have three different stories. Though we had some of the same experiences, this is my version of those experiences. Love you Moore!

To my children:

Tia because you are my first born and had to endure the learning curve of me becoming a parent.

Mia because you are so much like me, determined, ambitious yet enduring.

Donte because as my third child you showed me how hard I can work without even knowing you did.

Emmanuel, your name says it all. Without you, without God I wouldn't have progressed to be the person I am today.

To my grandchildren:

I hope one day you will read this and not judge your grandfather. Without him there'd be no you. And as you know, you all are my heart.

And know the strength and determination to succeed is in each of you. Keep God in your own way always a part of your life.

To my nieces and nephews

As the family historian you all call me. It reminded me why I had to start writing while I remember so much. I hope you see what your mother, my sister and your father, my brother, came from. They do have more details about their experiences, but this is a start. Love Aunt Gina

To my God mom, Ma Doris

You know parts of my story and as you read this you will know the depths I came from. Thank you for being there and setting some examples of motherhood I took to my children.

To my girlfriends

It's not enough room to name you all, however, to all who consistently encouraged me to complete this book. It only took a few decades, but most of you stayed with me. Thank you so much.

To my therapists

Without you by my side these last twelve years, I definitely would not have been able to emotionally handle writing and editing this book. Thank you!

To Lisa of Writer's Alley, I could not have completed this book without your editing, aid in writing and the mental support you provided. Thank you so much!

To Debbie, RIP....You would have been so proud!

FIRST BORN MIDDLE CHILD

TABLE OF CONTENTS

Prologue

"The only limit to the height of your achievements is the reach of your dreams and your willingness to work for them." —Michelle Obama

Nervously, waiting for my name to be announced. I can see the red Davenport University banner wave slightly behind the podium and hear the murmur of the crowd. It's Alumni Awards night for Davenport University, and I was selected to be the first recipient of the Perseverance Award. My heart is beating with triumphant energy, and I can feel a little trickle of sweat rolling down my back. On this night, everything seems to be moving in slow motion.

The Van Andel Museum is so big, a place for history and knowledge. Now the lobby is full of students, family, and faculty. I am standing near the stage with my kids and my sister, Yasmin. I hear the names and speeches of the awards recipients who are called before me. Dominic and Michael, 13 and 11 years old, are squirming in their shirts and ties, so I tell them they have to behave. Tia, 20, and Mia, 16, are brimming. Tia is a student at the University of Michigan.

Mia helped me pick out my dress. Shopping with her was wonderful, in spite of the racism we had to endure. We had tried to shop at an upscale boutique and waited to be helped for quite a while. When it was my turn to pay, the white lady who got there after us was helped first. I told Mia that we wouldn't be shopping there, placed the dresses I planned to buy on the counter, and we went across the street to JC Penney's and bought a dress with ease. This dress represents the confidence I now have to stand up for myself and the desire to be a role model for my daughter.

I listen as the president of the college, Brenda Mieras, speaks about this woman who knew education was her family's hope for a future, a woman who led a determined life focused on education, not only for herself, but also her children and siblings. It's as though my brain can't process

1

what is happening. But it's my name she calls, and I am ready.

My speech clenched in my hand; I walked to the podium. Like most people I am afraid of making speeches, but I feel thankful that I had the forethought to take public speaking in high school, knowing I would one day want to share my story. Truthfully, presenting myself to a crowd made up mostly of strangers is easier than what life has already put me through. Putting my life in front of people I know, in front of my friends, colleagues, and children--that is difficult. But I have found at this point that healing comes through being open and honest--with myself and others.

It's important that my dress is red. My entire upbringing, I was told that wearing red was a sign that a woman was inviting men to pay attention to her. I never wanted the attention men gave me, and I certainly didn't want to look as if I was asking for it. This has been a sacrifice because red is my favorite color. Wearing the red dress was my act of bravery, not only because I showed my daughter that we could walk away when we were being treated unfairly but because I deserve to wear what I like without worrying about being judged, without thinking that everyone will believe I deserve every bad thing that happened to me. I deserve the good things.

I still wonder why I was the first recipient of the Perseverance Award. I graduated with an associate degree in Computer Programming over eighteen years ago. The truth was I had only done what I had to for my children, my siblings, and my pride. I wished I had asked, "Why me?" when Brenda Mieras called me to ask if I could come to be recognized. What if this was a mistake or joke and I would be standing in front of everyone while they thought I was a fraud? I would not let myself dwell on that, so when I finished putting on makeup and doing my hair, I walked into the living room until it was time to leave.

I reassured myself by remembering how Brenda Mieras had wondered how they were going to get me and my kids to Michigan to accept this award. If they were willing to do that, they must be serious. I had recently worked at Home Depot at corporate headquarters in Atlanta. Thankfully, I had returned to Michigan and was working in Information Technology at Meijer Incorporated, the mid-western grocery store chain. I reminded myself of another fact: not only had I gotten two excellent jobs, but jobs also weren't usually possible for black women. The State of Michigan that had fed and clothed me when I was a child was not going to do the same for my children. I had a moment of thinking that I actually deserve this award--I have persevered through so much. I think about the time when my dad told me my biological mother was African. I later learned it was in my blood to persevere through a lot because of my African heritage. The word for that in Yoruba is **ifarada** *or* **Perseverance.**

Now, as I stand at the podium, I make myself think good thoughts about my accomplishments, allowing those feelings to sink in so that I can deliver my speech and feel like I deserve the life I have built, despite everything. Even though feeling a little comfort and love were things I longed for every minute of my childhood, not something I knew could be freely given and taken for granted. I was seventeen the first time I ever really celebrated a birthday, and I did it with a cake I bought for myself with only my one-year-old, my sister, and brother to share it with. In my life, I had lived through abandonment, fear, sexual abuse, hunger, physical punishment, pregnancy, uncertainty, and denial of my name and family.

This is the story of the first twenty years of my life. Of why I believed I deserved this award and became remembered by the president of my alma mater as the student who succeeded against extreme odds.

Chapter 1
What I've Learned about My Early Years

"As black women, we're always given these seemingly devastating experiences — experiences that could absolutely break us. But what the caterpillar calls the end of the world, [God] calls the butterfly. What we do as black women is take the worst situations and create from that point." —Viola Davis

I was born in 1963 in Boston, Massachusetts, to a mobster and his girlfriend. Their tumultuous relationship ended in Simi Valley, California, in 1968 just after I entered preschool. I only know the bare outlines of these early years from stories my daddy told me when I was allowed to visit him as a child. At one point my adoptive father beat me and refused to let me see my daddy again because I had the nerve to talk back. The rest of my early experiences would have to wait until I was old enough to contact my daddy again—and I'd learn just a little more. Piecing together the story of my childhood and why my life went the way it did, searching for answers and love, became the project of my early adulthood.

I can't remember what I called my mother. For the life of me I just can't. I referred to her as She, whether I was talking to somebody else or in my own thoughts. My daddy would refer to her as Jade or "your mother," so I know that is who she was, but throughout my life I could not associate a motherly name or role to her—that might have been because of the trauma that I feel she caused by abandoning me. For years, I would ask two questions. "Will she come back?" After a while I started to think "Since she doesn't love me than why would anyone else?"

From stories I pieced together, I know my parents met in Washington, D.C. My dad had left Detroit to hide from the mafia. Jade (my mother) had only her youngest daughter, Kim, with her when they met. They thought they had settled in our nation's capital, Washington D.C., permanently until the mafia found them. She was about seven months pregnant with me, and if things had gone differently that night, I wouldn't have been born.

4

Suddenly, they moved together to Boston. I don't know why they chose Boston. Was it because it was an East Coast mafia haven? But that is where I was born prematurely. I wasn't born into poverty, and my early years were comfortable and even affluent. That's something that seems to surprise a lot of people.

I don't remember much about our lives there. In Boston, my daddy played poker with mobsters he told me. That he won his business, painting houses from a player that lost to him. Somehow this made me think that he must own Benjamin Moore Paints in the commercials I seen. Because even at three years old, I knew my name was Moore. My daddy always said he wanted me to know who I was and where I came from. Later, it would seem like the whole world was trying to take that away from me, but I have always clung to my name. My dad told me this story, but not the rest. It wasn't until I was an adult that I learned just what they meant by "painting houses." To the mob, painting meant only one thing, painting the walls with someone's blood. My dad was a hitman. He eventually admitted that to me, though I never wanted to know the details.

Despite this, by the time I was eight, my dad would tell me stories about his killings. He told me about a man who owed him money. My dad said he strung him upside down on a pole and shot him. He acted like all of this was normal, talking about it the same way he talked about driving a mail truck. He said the army had taught him to kill, and he had been forced to do whatever was needed to survive. He had a tin of awards from his service, including a Purple Heart. As a sharpshooter in the army, my dad had killed a lot of people and saved a lot of people. He didn't seem to see the difference.

Dad told me we lived in Boston for almost three years. Then Jade wanted to sing professionally, so we moved to Northridge, California, a suburb in Los Angeles County. My brother was born in LA while my sister Yasmin was born in Hollywood ten months later. Yes, Hollywood, on purpose. Jade liked the glam life and was determined to become a famous singer. She loved anything to do with fame, and she even named my baby sister after an actress in the hospital when she gave birth.

My dad bought their home in Northridge but hit it big in Vegas. He then purchased a mansion in Simi Valley, California, next to Stanley Davis, Jr. When I was an adult, daddy told me he couldn't understand why Jade left him. She not only had a mansion; she had a maid to take care of all the work. He admitted he used the house in Northridge as a brothel, but he also worked third shift driving a double semi for the post office to make sure he could give her the money to pay the bills. He left out the part of why she really left him.

The first big event I remember is going to private school in Simi Valley. At that time, when you went to school, even preschool, you got your vaccinations on the first day. My dad and I rode to school in a big car with the girl who lived next door and her daddy. I didn't know her daddy was famous, so I just knew her as Tina. I was bubbling with excitement for my first day of school. My sister, Kim, already went to school, and I thought, "Now I get to go, too". We passed all the big pretty houses, some with walls or gates around them, some in the plain open. We soon arrived at the building with a big pink wall around it. The driver opened our door. Tina and Kim were older and knew exactly what to do, so they went to play. I got out of the car with my daddy. We walked up to the school and into the building, me holding my dad's hand because I was so attached to him. As my dad walked me into the big white building, I became a bit shy. So many kids all dressed alike. A lady dressed in white takes my hand.

"Daddy, you aren't going to leave me, are you?" At five, I was closest to my daddy. He's the one who took care of me and my siblings during the day while Jade was busy trying to become famous. When I was an adult, he told me that my sister and brother and I were his last chance to have a family, and I was the first child of his last chance.

He responded, "No, Regina I'm here." Somehow knowing I had my daddy made me feel safe, so when the nurse said she had to give me a shot and pointed to a small room, I was willing to go. I went into the room and the nurse pinched my left shoulder and stuck a needle in it. I cried out, "Daddy." The nurse said, "He's gone, and you are going to play with the other kids." I didn't believe her because he said he would wait. When I came back out, he was gone, though.

I cried and asked her, "Where did my daddy go?" She repeated that he had to leave so I could play with the other kids. I didn't want to play with other kids. I wanted my daddy. I can't remember ever feeling so sad and lonely. It seems like there's a big empty hole in my tummy.

This was my first experience of abandonment, but it certainly wasn't the last. Looking back, it seems like such a small incident given everything else I would eventually go through. But this is my last memory of my daddy in Simi Valley, California, and for all I know, it was almost the last time I had my daddy before she took us away.

The nurse ushered me out to where more kids were playing on the playground. My friend Tina was there. So, I ran to her. She was crying, too, so I wiped my tears, and I hugged her. Her daddy was gone, too. I guessed that was just what daddies do. This was my first experience with what would become normal for me--adults hurting and abandoning me. Eventually I would learn that my daddy wasn't the man I thought he was, but he remained the most consistent adult in my life, even when he wasn't around. I can't say why, but I would continue to seek him out throughout my life in the hopes of experiencing his unquestionable love for me. Until I was eight, or maybe I just wasn't old enough to realize it.

By the time I was five, Jade decided to leave my dad, and we went to her mom's. Who told us to leave. However, before we pulled away from her house in Virginia, Mama Baxter came to me, "Remember this address," she said. She gave me her address and I repeated it back to her three times.

The drive to New York was long, and I watched the trees and looked up to the sky and repeated the address over and over. It felt somehow like remembering it was a connection to Mama Baxter. Over the next years when I couldn't sleep, I would repeat that address, my form of counting sheep. I knew it was a place I may never see, even when I wanted to go anyplace else, but it was a link, and I needed every connection I could find, fleeting, inaccessible—it didn't matter.

Even though I have an extraordinary memory for details, I know all of this is perceived through the eyes of my childhood. I know what happened henceforth, because I lived it, not because someone told me about it later. *Now I can tell my story as I experienced it, the way I remember it.*

Chapter 2

No More School

"People expect all stories of abuse to be loud and angry but they're not. Sometimes they're quiet and cruel and swept under the rug."— Trista Mateer, Aphrodite Made Me Do It

Uncle David isn't with us anymore. He was funny and I miss him. I woke up in a new place. *She* tells us this is where Fred lives. Fred isn't funny. *She* says he's Kim 's dad. We used to play a game in preschool where you put things that are alike together. I can do this with my family. I look different from Kim, even though we are sisters. My skin is darker than Kim's. Junior and I are more like Jade. Yasmin is like Fred and Kim. Maybe that is why Fred treats me and Junior differently from the others. In the mornings, Fred pushes Junior and me out the door as soon as Jade leaves for work and Kim goes to school. We play on the balcony that goes around the building. Junior and I are hungry, and Fred doesn't let us come in during the day. We find the milk and orange juice at people's door that had just been delivered in the morning before the neighbors come out to get it, and we drink it. After the neighbors complain, Fred gets mad and yells at us for stealing.

We have lived here a while, but I don't know how long. This is our new life now. Fred starts to put me and Junior in the living room closet every day after Jade goes to work. Fred says it's because we are bad and made the neighbors mad. I sit in the dark, hugging my brother, peeking through the small crack in the locked door where light comes in. It's just a little bit of light, but I tell Junior at least we aren't in the dark.

I try to make up games so Junior doesn't cry in the scariness of that closet, where long woolen coats hang over our heads. It smells like old shoes and something wet, like a washrag that you leave out on the counter for too many days. Junior cries sometimes because he's just two and a half, and he wants to run and play, he wants food, he wants love. I'm five, so it's my job to take care of him. I say let's pretend we're in the woods. We pretend we can run around outside. I sing songs and try to teach him the alphabet and other things I learned in preschool. But school was a long time ago in the other place where I lived with my daddy. I wish I was in school. Now instead of school, I stay in the closet with Junior.

The closet is in the corner of the apartment, next to the front door. When I peep through the crack, I see Yasmin sitting on the bed playing with Fred. He is tickling her, and they laugh together. He changes her diaper and brings her into the main part of the apartment to give her food. It's after her first birthday, but we don't celebrate birthdays like the other kids in my preschool. Just talk about when they happen. Why does she get to play with him while me and Junior stay in the closet? He treats her and Kim like he's their daddy, but he treats me and Junior like strangers. Yasmin is happy, and I never hear her crying the way Junior does, whimpering in the darkness. I'm glad she is happy, but I still feel bad for Junior inside.

Most days, Junior and I fall asleep. The click of the lock wakes us up, and we are always out of the closet when it's time for Jade to get home. I am so scared of Fred and know I can't talk about the closet. Jade plays with Yasmin for a few minutes and tells Kim to do her homework. She doesn't talk to Junior and me much, so I don't tell her anything. One day, Fred falls asleep with Yasmin in his room, and he never comes to let us out of the closet. The front door clicks and Jade walks in. Junior calls out to her, before I can hush him. She removes the chair that's against the closet door, and the light comes in, bright and blinding. Junior and me cover our eyes and blink until we get used to the light. *She* doesn't hug us or comfort us. Instead, *she* looks in her bedroom and sees Fred sleeping curled up with Yasmin.

Then I hear the yelling. I can't hear what she is saying. I can't hear what he yells back. I just hear anger. Maybe we won't have to go back in the closet.

Next thing I know Kim is on the floor crying, while Jade talks to her. "I'll be back but your sisters and brother won't be." I don't understand what she is talking about, but Kim keeps crying. "Don't take them," she says. Take who? I wonder. Her father tells her to shut up.

But then *she* takes Junior, Yasmin, and me away. Kim stays with her daddy, with Fred, who isn't as mean to her as he is to me. Jade doesn't say where we are going or why we are leaving, but I know. I shouldn't have opened the neighbors' milk and orange juice. I cry now, knowing I am leaving Kim, even though I am happy to be away from Fred. I wipe my tears as Junior reaches for me. I sat down on the ground in front of the apartment building and grabbed him onto my lap and started wiping his tears, just like I did in the closet so many days. He stops crying. I held him close and rocked him back and forth. I look up to Jade holding my sister. Yasmin is sleeping. I wish I could hold her too. It's just us. No daddy. No Kim or Fred. Junior and I sit there while *she* gets the car and puts Yasmin in it. I'm five.

Chapter 3

First Time at Grandmo's

"The family drama may look and sound different from generation to generation, but all toxic patterns are remarkably similar in their outcome: pain and suffering."
— Susan Forward, Toxic Parents: Overcoming Their Hurtful Legacy and Reclaiming Your Life

Then the train ride. The mountains are so big, as I look out my window. The train moves so fast. I wish it would slow down so I could look more at the mountains. There are so many of them. Tall, some with trees growing out of them. Lots of green. The world outside changes every time the train goes clickety click. As it starts to get dark, I look across the seat from me where Yasmin is sitting in *her* lap fast asleep. Junior is sitting next to me also asleep. I can't close my eyes. I am so excited because I think we are going back to Daddy. I'm Daddy's girl. I am afraid to ask *her* if we are going to see daddy, so instead I just ask, "When do we get off the train?"

She answers, "Soon. Don't ask again." I ask every time the train stops, and each time I get the same answer. Eventually even I get tired of the question and start to sleep through the train ride.

Suddenly the train stops, bouncing me awake. Outside the window I see other trains and a sign that says Coney Island. I can read the words because of the letters I learned in school. I haven't forgotten. Pictures of hot dogs are on the sign, too. It looks like a restaurant; I know because we went to some when we were driving with Uncle David. "Can we have a hot dog? Junior and baby?"

"Calm down, Regina," *she* says in her mean voice. Then we stood up and slowly left the train. There are so many people I feel like we might get crushed, and I can't see anything but the backs of their legs. "Grab Junior's hand and stay close," *she* says. I follow her to a table in the hot dog place. "Sit here while I get the hot dogs."

I smell cooked hot dogs, and I hope she remembers I like mustard on mine, not ketchup. She puts the food in front of me and tells me to share with Junior then starts walking away with Yasmin on her hip. "Where are you going?" I ask.

"Over to that phone booth. Now, watch your brother." I eat my hot dog even though it has ketchup. When *she* comes back, *she* says, "Hurry and finish your food, we need to go."

"Are we going to see Daddy?"

"No, we're going to your grandmother's."

"Mama Baxter?" I have only met her one time, but she is the only grandmother I know.

"No, *your* grandma," she says. I don't understand. Mama Baxter is my grandmother. But *she* doesn't let me ask anything else and we hustle into a yellow car. We pass some tall buildings then turn onto a street with house after house. Some are big, and some are small. They have scrabbly trees and grass in front of them, and the paint colors look faded. None of the houses is as big or as pretty as my daddy's house. But it's better than New York. I wonder who lives in all these places and which one we are going to. Will Daddy be there? The yellow car stops in front of this big yellow house. *She* says, "Go ahead, get out." I get out first then grab Junior's hand. She holds the baby in her arms. We walk up to the porch where a gray-haired lady and two other ladies are sitting. I see kids who look my age playing in the yard.

"Hi, I'm Jade," *she* says to the gray-haired lady. "This is Regina, she's five, and Junior is two, and Yasmin." *She* hands Yasmin to the old lady and looks at me, "Regina, this is your grandmother." *She* looks at the lady, "What do they call you?"

"Grandmo is fine." All the ladies on the porch are looking at us, and I don't like the way it makes me feel. I thought we were going to see daddy, and *She* brought us to this place. Why?

"Where's daddy?" I ask. I'm almost crying.

"This is your daddy's mama, your other grandmother." Then *she* reaches into her purse and hands me some money. "You and Junior go with your cousins to the store across the street to get some candy." I instantly got so excited. I love candy. I am a big girl, with a lot of money, and I am going to be in charge of all the kids. I think about what I might buy.

Boston Baked Beans are my favorite and Fritos, too, even if they aren't candy. Junior loves Now-n-Laters.

Still holding his hand, me, Junior, and my new cousins hurried toward the store. It's just across the street and a few houses away. In the store, I say, "Wow, so much candy." I got the Now-n-Laters and a bag of Fritos and a box of Boston Baked Beans. I give the man at the counter my money, smiling. I am so excited that I don't even see what my cousins are doing. I give Junior his Now-n-Laters while grabbing his other hand, and we all head out of the store. As we cross the street, he slips from my hand and runs into the street. A yellow car like the one we came here in stops with a screeching noise. I grabbed Junior's hand again.

"Don't run away from me," I say to him in my mean voice, just like *her*. As we walked away from the yellow car, I looked up. *She* is in the back seat of that car, her head turned away from us. I freeze. *She* doesn't look up no matter how hard I stare at her. The yellow car drives away. I stand in the street with Junior watching until it becomes far away. I wonder, "Is *she* gone? Why didn't *she* wait for us? Is baby with *her*?" I don't even remember what I called *her,* what I called out to her. But I know I'm supposed to be with *her*, and something is really wrong. Now I'm not going to be with my daddy or with my mother.

I ran with a tight grip on Junior's hand to the porch of the yellow house. I ask the gray-haired lady who I just met, "Where is the lady that brought me here?" I forgot I was supposed to call her Grandmo.

Grandmo answers, "Baby, you gonna be okay." What did that even mean? I was ok before I went into the store. I'm not okay *now*.

I ask again, "Where *she* go?" She just says again that I'll be alright. Another lady on the porch is holding my baby sister. My brother started crying. Where is my bag of Fritos or Boston Baked Beans? Did I drop them? Did my brother drop his? Is it in the street? Did the taxi run over my candy? He wants his candy, and I am hurting his hand, squeezing it so tight. One of the other ladies reaches for my brother and sits him on her lap to rock him. Grandmo reaches for me, but I yank back. I don't want to sit in anyone's lap. I want the lady in the yellow car to come back and get us and take us back to Daddy. "When is *she* coming back to get us?" I yell.

The Grandmo lady says again, "Baby, you gonna be okay. And call me Grandmo." I can't call her anything. I started crying.

"Where's daddy?" I ask again.

"I don't know, but you are going to be alright." These people *she* left me with, I don't know. All I know is my little brother and my sister and I are alone. I'm only five. Is it my fault? Why, why, why did my she leave, and my daddy's not here? Daddy will call us at Grandmo's, right? Will *she* call us, too? This strange place is so big and scary and now we are all alone, except for these strange people. I am not supposed to go with strangers, but that is all there is.

Grandmo turns to my aunts to tell me their names. "This here is your aunt Niecy," she says, pointing to the big lady holding the baby.

"Hi Regina, you have long braids," Niecy says.

I say, "Thank you." Daddy always said, to say thank you when people talk about my hair.

The small lady who is holding Junior says, "Call me Aunt Karen and that's my daughter Ava," in a rough voice and points to the light-skin girl sitting on the porch step eating her candy. "Y'all are the same age."

Aunt Niecy interrupts to add her daughter Gabrielle is also the same age. Grandmo says to me, "These are your daddy's sisters. Your other aunts Sharon and Danielle don't live here."

I think, "Who cares?" But I know I can't say that, so I nod. These people are strangers to me, and they look so different from my dad and me that I don't feel like they have anything to do with me. My dad is tall with light brown skin and wavy hair. He is strong and handsome. These people are darker than him and *strange* looking. They are not like the women my dad knew in California who were fancy dressed. Those are the people I'm used to. My grandmother and one aunt wears house dresses with aprons and tennis shoes. My dad always wears the best clothes. My dad was big-time. This place, which I later learned is called Jackson, Michigan, feels like a pretty small place. I hate it here, and I hate everyone.

Except Yasmin and Junior. I love them. I have to make sure they are okay.

My two younger aunts dress more for the streets--*she* used to say that, but I don't know what it means. The lady called Aunt Sharon comes over after we have been there a while. She asks, "Do you remember me?"

"No, ma'am," I answer.

"I came to Boston to babysit you. It was before your brother and sister were born."

I am excited for a minute, thinking she must know where daddy is, so I ask her, "Do you know where my daddy is now?"

"He's in California, I think."

"Do you know when the lady is coming back to get us?"

She ignores my question and instead goes on to say, "You look just like your mama." I started to cry again and rock Junior harder and harder. I'm supposed to be a big girl, and I'm supposed to be polite, but I don't care about these people. I want to go with *her* and back to Daddy.

Grandmo says, "Baby you gonna be okay." I am starting to feel mad every time she says that. I am not alright. It is not good to be here, and I don't even know where I will sleep or where my stuff is or what is going to happen to us. Grandmo tells me that my aunt Karen and her two kids Ava and Theo live there too. And that my aunt Danielle is not here but Grandmo points to her kids, Regina, and Maddox in the yard. "They live here too."

"Regina? That's my name," I say, surprise making me stop crying for a minute.

Grandmo says, "We call her Gigi, and so we'll call you Jean-Jean." I like Regina, my real name.

That same night Grandmo yells "BEDTIME!" and tells me and Junior to go upstairs with my cousins. Someone points to a bed and tells me that's where I'm going to sleep. It seems like this is going to be my home, but that isn't right. I have a different home at my daddy's, and even if I haven't been there for a while, I'm sure my daddy is waiting for me to come back. Once he finds out where we are, he is going to rush right over and get us. Junior crawls in bed next to me, and that is some comfort. Grandmo brings Yasmin and lays her next to us. Junior starts crying and I hold him close. I want to cry too, but I can't. Just like in the closet, I have to make him feel better. I have to be strong for Junior and Yasmin

He soon cries himself to sleep. Yasmin was already asleep. I start thinking: Why did *she* leave us? What did I do? Didn't *she* love us? *She* must not. So, then nobody will. Why didn't Kim come with us? Who are these people? I never heard of them, and *she* is just going to leave me with them. What do I know about my daddy's relatives when all I know is her, daddy, Kim, Uncle David, and Mama Baxter? Fred doesn't count. These people are not going to love me. Why would they?

There is a what feels like hole in my chest. A big hole. It hurts. Now that Junior and Yasmin are asleep, I can only cry and cry. But the pain won't go away. It's there no matter how many times this Grandmo says I'll be alright. Alright, is seeing *her* and my daddy. Where is daddy? Why did we leave our house? Such a long ride I don't know how we could ever get back. It was *her*, Kim, Yasmin, Junior and my Uncle David. I remember Mama Baxter telling me the address to memorize. I repeat it over and over through my tears: 803 E Saint Mark Street, Petersburg, Virginia, 23803. Why did she tell me to do this? She knew I was going away…away? Where? Why? Didn't Mama Baxter love me too? If there's nobody left who loves you, what happens to you? Sobbing, I fall asleep. My first night with people I do not know.

Chapter 4

Back to School

"I've always loved the first day of school better than the last day of school. Firsts are best because they are beginnings."—Jenny Han, author.

When I wake up one morning, I'm excited remembering Grandmo said I get to go to school. I ran downstairs. Junior and Yasmin are already there. After I eat breakfast, Grandmo says go get washed up and dressed for school. I go into the bathroom where my cousins, Ava and Gigi, fight over the sink. They are splashing and calling each other names, but I wait my turn quietly. They act like I'm not there. I need to show Grandmo that I'm not any trouble, that she doesn't need to lock me in a closet or punish me to keep me behaving. Ready for school, I wait for her to approve. She nods in a way that makes me think she likes how I look and says, "I'm going to walk all you kids to school today."

"I usually go to school in a big, long car," I tell her.

"Well, we're walking," she says. I kiss Junior and Yasmin goodbye. Yasmin crawls around the floor and doesn't seem to know that I'm leaving. Junior knows it will be the first time we are apart in a long time. Since I went to school with daddy. I'm sad for leaving him but I'm too excited about going to school.

"I'll be back soon," I tell them. Junior starts to cry. "Don't cry. I'm coming back. I have to go to school." My aunt picks him up to distract him as we go out the door. As we start walking, I ask Grandmo, for about the hundredth time, "When is *she* coming back to get us?"

"Baby, you gonna be okay," she says again.

"Why do you always say that?" I ask. She looks at me sternly. I shut up and looks down. Her answer makes me mad but I can't tell her that. Instead, I try to figure out what will happen by myself. Once daddy finds out where we are, he will come to get us. Daddy loves me and his job is to take care of me, not Grandmo or those aunts I don't know. They acted nice at first, but now one of then just yells. The aunts say everything we do is bad. Yasmin and Junior are always in trouble. I try to be good enough to make up for them, so we can stay here until my daddy comes to find us. Sometimes I wonder what if Grandmo sends us back to Fred. I would see Kim, and maybe *she* would be there. But *she* took us away from there and left us here, so it doesn't seem like going back would be good. Now that we're living with Aunt Karen, it's like going from one mean person to another. I hope Junior and Yasmin are okay while I am at school.

Grandmo doesn't answer about why she says it's alright when it isn't, and nobody says anything else until we get to school. It's a really, really big school. I have to bend my head way back to see the top of the building. It has lots of windows.

"Will I get lost in there?" I asked my cousin, Gigi. She tells me it will be alright and that we get to play outside and have fun. Sometimes Gigi is nice to me because we have the same name. Ava and Gigi and me can be friends, even though they are my cousins.

Grandmo leaves my cousins on the playground and walks me to the principal's office. I sit in a chair trying not to fidget while Grandmo tells this man that she is my grandmother, her daddy's mother.

"Her mother dropped her off. She's five and was going to preschool in California before they came here." I was so excited to be at school until I heard Grandmo talk about me being left at her house. I started to cry. Where is *she*? When is *she* coming back? And daddy, he was always in the car taking me to school. When will he come to get me? Grandma turns toward me and says, "Baby, you gonna be okay." I ball my hands into fists. I want to hit something, but that isn't what a good girl would do, so I make the anger stay inside me until it becomes an ache in my tummy, something I can feel but nobody else can see.

The tall man Grandmo was talking to tells me his name is Mr. Green. He says, "I'm going to take you to your new teacher." I wipe my tears because I don't want my new teacher to not like me. School is a good place, so I will be happy here, I think. At my school in Simi Valley, grown-ups always smiled after I answered their questions. I hope it will be the same here.

18

I am in Mrs. James's kindergarten class. When I get into the classroom, she asks me if I can count to ten. I nod my head up and down and count all the way to a hundred.

"Wow, you really can count. Now let's work on your colors," Mrs. James says. I know the name of every color she shows me. Mrs. James smiles with happiness, and I think I am going to like this school. "You're such a smart girl," she says. I love being in a place where I can shine, where nobody tells me that I'm not good, that I don't know something. The kids aren't as kind as the teacher, and they pick on me for talking proper. "You sound like a white girl," they say—the same thing my cousins said after meeting me the first day.

During the day, we do our coloring or letters, take a nap, and get to play on the playground, my favorite part. The mats are rolled and stacked in neat pyramids, a word I have just learned. There are cubbies for boots, and each kid gets one, with a name tag to show who is whose. Mine is Regina, a name nobody calls me around here, but it's what my daddy calls me. The teacher says everything is supposed to be orderly, and I like that. I like knowing my cubby is the second one from the top, that it has my stuff in it, and nobody is supposed to touch it. This is different from Grandmo's house, where everybody lives and all their stuff is everywhere, and nothing is really mine.

When the bell rings, it's time to go home. I'm sad because I can't tell daddy or *her* how exciting school is to me. I think kindergarten is even better than preschool. We get to learn more stuff, and the teacher always smiles when I raise my hand. It feels so good when she tells me I'm smart—nobody at Grandmo's says anything nice like that—and even though my Aunt Karen says I'm not special, I know being smart is good, and I like it. I wish I could tell them because maybe then they would want to keep me, maybe they would love me better and not make me live with these people. But instead of daddy in the big, long car, my cousins are waiting for me outside the school. They call me over, with a "Hey, Jean-Jean," and we walk together back to Grandmo's house.

I start to feel like this is really my life. Between school and playing with my cousins, I don't miss *her* as much. But bedtimes are always so hard. Each night Grandmo yells, "BEDTIME!" and we all know to head upstairs because she

19

isn't going to say it a second time. I'm the only one who dares delay for a second, and it's so I can ask her, "When is *she* coming to get us? Where's Daddy?" Grandmo always says the same thing, "Baby, you gonna be okay." She doesn't call me Jean-Jean or Regina then, only baby. I guess she thinks it'll make me feel better. But it doesn't. I don't know why she doesn't tell my daddy that we are here so he will come to get us.

I can't remember what I called *her.* Mom, Mama, Ma, Mother? I don't remember, only remember seeing her leave in that yellow car with the white light on top. She looked down, never up, to see me or even say good-bye. Why didn't she say bye? Because she was coming back, right? But she didn't. She didn't even tell me I was going to live with these people. She just left. Sent me and Junior to the store to buy candy. Candy. Was it going to make me feel better? Should it make me feel better? I try to be a big girl and not think about this, but it keeps coming back in my head and I can't stop it, not for a long time. Even when I'm not thinking about it, the feeling stays will me, sadness so deep I think that if I looked down there would be a hole that goes right through me.

A lot of people live at Grandmo's house and even more come to stay there during the days. It takes me a long time to figure out who everyone is. Nobody is akin to me, except Yasmin and Junior, that is something I know for sure. I have two uncles, along with all the aunts. Uncle Billy lives there. He's very quiet. He looks like my daddy, but he doesn't act like my daddy. He just goes to work and comes home—he never talks or plays with us kids.

My Uncle Tommy lives here, tall and skinny, and my cousins say he's only daddy's half-brother. He pays some attention to the kids, but he says I'm his special girl. He never plays the kissing game with Ava or Gigi. It's only me he sits on his lap with my legs straddled around him. I'm facing him, and he says he'll teach me how to kiss. He kisses me on my mouth, pulling me toward him on his lap, and tells me, "This is how you kiss." It feels messy and a lot of spit is on my lips, but he says, "That's a good job." Just like in school, I learned to do it right, and that makes me feel good, even if I don't really like the kissing part or the way his stubble picks my skin and makes me feel yucky.

One time, Grandmo walks in the room and catches us. She yells, "Tommy, get that girl off your lap! Right now, get her off!" I know right away that there is something wrong. Is it me, I wonder? I like feeling special, playing this game with Uncle Tommy. He's a grownup, so I'm supposed to do what he says. The next time, he says we must be careful that Grandmo doesn't see us. She doesn't like kissing. It must be wrong since Grandmo yelled. But Uncle Tommy sits me on his lap, and I let him pull me toward him to pop a little kiss on my lips whenever he asks. I'm not supposed to say no to a grownup.

Grandpa lives in Grandmo's house, too. I know I'm supposed to call him Grandpa, but he isn't really mine. My cousin, Ava, Karen's daughter, tells me all the time, "He's not your grandpa, just mine." Sometimes Ava isn't nice to me. She smiles a nasty smile when she goes to play with her grandpa and I can't go, too. I don't want to play with Grandpa, but I want somebody who is mine, and he isn't, says Ava. She's right, Grandmo says he's my dad's stepfather, which means he's not really my kin. Grandpa is gone a lot and never says much when he is here, except to play with Ava. I wish my daddy was here to play with me. One night, Grandpa comes in smelling foul, and Grandmo gets really mad at him and starts yelling. She runs into the kitchen and comes back into the living room with a knife, trying to stab him. My aunts heard the commotion and yelled at Grandmo to stop. She yells that she isn't going to stop because Grandpa had spent his money getting drunk. To me he always smells like that.

At Grandmo's house, everybody always argues, teases, and fights, but sometimes things feel okay. There are times when I am happy, like going to my Aunt Niecy's house. She has six kids and one of them, Gabrielle, is my age. I love to play with Gabrielle and go to their house because we can go down the street to the school playground. We can play on that merry-go-round, my favorite. When it's just us, Gabrielle doesn't tease me, and Aunt Niecy doesn't yell like the other aunts. I usually get to go when Grandmo is at work, and we are not in school, but in the summer, I have more time to play and that is fun, even more fun than school, I think. I'm sad when kindergarten is over and I don't get to see Mrs. James anymore, but I will get to play outside. And next year I will be a first grader, and then I will really be in school, all day.

Also, at first, I like when I go fishing with Grandmo, just her and me because it's summer vacation. The part I don't like is I have to sit very quietly because Grandmo says if you talk then the fish gets scared away. I started to hate fishing because I can't talk, and I want to talk and learn. I want to be around people who love me. But fishing is where I learn to have what Grandmo calls patience. I also learned how to put a worm called bait on the fishing hook. Minutes pass while I sit there quietly next to Grandmo as she throws the rod back and forth. When her rod bends a fish is hooked. It hate the worm I put on it. Grandmo catches a few so I hold the bucket of water while she puts the fish in there. They plop all around and she tells me to put a lid on it and make sure that they don't get out. My job is to be quiet and follow all her orders. I'm not allowed to play with the fish in the bucket or wander off to look at anything. It seems like hours out there fishing. It isn't fair that my cousins are allowed to stay home and play, and I have to go fishing. My brother and sister get to stay home and play, too, but they are probably getting whippings if something goes wrong for sure. They are always so happy to see me when I get back, maybe because I try to protect them. And I am even happier to see them, but I don't get to play until I help clean the fish when we get home. Grandmo does the slicing with the knife because she is a good cook, that's her job, but I have to take out the guts and the bones. I hate it when I eat fish, and I swallow a bone. Grandmo says I will learn to do a better job. When a bone gets caught in your throat, they give you a slice of light bread to push it down. Then one of the aunts tells me not to eat so fast.

When summer is over, Grandmo walks me to school on the first day of first grade and says Mrs. Schiklen will be my teacher and that she is nice. Mrs. Schiklen is short and stout, that's a word I just learned, with a big smile and short hair. Even though all the teachers in Simi Valley were white, I had never seen anyone who looked like Mrs. Robertson. She is older, but not as old as Grandmo. She hugs all the students when we come in. She makes me feel good. I feel safe in school, and I still can make the teacher smile by showing her all the things I know. The teachers act like I'm smarter than most of the other kids in the class, and that makes me happy. They have their parents, most of them, so at least I have this. Sometimes I think daddy isn't going to come to get us. Why won't Grandmo call and tell him where we are? If she did, I know my daddy would come right away. We are just kids, and we should have a grownup who is ours who takes care of us. I don't know what will happen if we never have our family. Will we stay at Grandmo's forever? The aunts don't like us being there, I think, so maybe they should call daddy and tell him to come and get us. Sometimes I'm sad because I haven't seen him in so long that I'm scared I won't remember what he looks like.

Afternoons we walk the six blocks home from school, my cousin Ava and sometimes Gigi. Most of the houses we pass are just like Grandmo's, with an upstairs and a downstairs, front porches, and small green patches of grass in front. I know there are probably backyards with gardens, and maybe some kids and their toys. There are old cars in front, and even though nothing is shiny and new, it's not so bad. When I get home, Grandmo has chores for me to do. She doesn't have time to do everything for everyone because she says she has to go to work some days. She is the cook at a restaurant, one that is too fancy for us to go to. When she comes home, she says she is tired from standing up all day over a hot stove. That's why she needs me to help her all the time. There are a lot of people to take care of, and nobody else I see doing it.

It's during the week, so no fishing. I have to work in her garden or wash dishes. I am sad that I don't get to play when my cousins do, but they have parents who tell Grandmo they don't have to help. I don't have anybody, and I have to make sure that Grandmo will keep me and Junior and Yasmin. Grandmo has a big garden—apple trees, grapevines, veggies like tomatoes, onions, and greens. Most days, I have to help pick the vegetables, Grandmo calls them, and it takes me all the way until dinner and then bed sometimes. I pick the food, but there is still never enough. The table is crowded, and everyone is talking, and laughing, and grabbing food. The aunts make sure to fill up their kids' plates, but we don't have a mom to do that, and Grandmo is far away down the table. Most of the time, I am hungry, and I try to make sure Yasmin and Junior have something to eat so they won't be hungry, too. When I can get to the food, I make sure to scoop some onto their plates.

Some days if Grandmo is still at work when we get home from school, I get to watch *Spiderman* and *Batman* with all the kids. Robin is my favorite because his name starts with an R, like my real name. Spiderman is my favorite too because he wears my favorite color, red.

I'm six and a half and I know a lot of things. But I don't know where my daddy is. It seems like Grandmo should know because he is her son. When I ask Grandmo to call daddy she says she has to wait for him to call. I don't know why, and she doesn't explain. Doesn't daddy know where we are, yet? Why won't Grandmo call and tell him? It takes a lot of days for daddy to call, months even. I am in first grade now, so I know it is a long time. I haven't forgotten about my daddy, but I have to make myself remember fun times with him to remember him. To me, he is a hero, like Batman—and my daddy is rich and has a fancy car too—who wouldn't have left us here or let bad things happen to us, not like *her.*

Then Daddy calls! Grandmo talks to him for a little while, and I stay nearby, thinking maybe I can hear his voice. It's finally my turn to talk. I don't tell him about the kissing game or the teasing or even the whippings that Yasmin and Junior get. I just ask when he is coming to get me, to get us.

"When will I see you? Are you coming to get us? Will you be here soon?" I ask, using my polite voice, so daddy will remember what a good girl I am and want to take me home.

"Slow down, Regina," he says. "There's nobody here to watch you while I go to work." Then I ask when *she* is coming back. He says, "I don't know, but no matter what happens, you have to love your mother." I think I am going to cry when daddy says, "I can't take care of you right now, but my mama will take good care of you."

"But, daddy, I miss you. Yasmin and Junior miss you, too."

"I miss you, too. Put your Grandmo back on the phone." I try to hear what they are saying, but Grandmo turns her back to me and talks really low. I see her talking on the phone like that other times and wonder if she is talking to my daddy, but I don't always get to talk, too. I wonder if all the other times before now when I've seen her talking like this if she has been talking to my daddy. That can't be right because then he would have come to get us after the first call. Sometimes he calls again, and I get to talk to daddy. I am learning about days and weeks and months in school, but I don't know how often he calls or when it will be.

At least I have Mrs. Schiklen. She is so nice, and I like the way school goes the same way every day. She hugs me in the mornings when I get there. I think this is what a real mom would do. Sometimes I even see my cousins' getting hugs at home, and now I know what it would feel like. We are practicing our writing, and Mrs. Schiklen walks around the room to check on everybody. I am so happy when she stops at my desk to tell me I am doing a good job. I try to make my letters neat, so she will notice. Mrs. Schiklen says good handwriting is important. It's almost like drawing pictures, and I love to do that, too. When I am at school, it's like I am a whole different person who people like and who is good.

The whole year goes by so fast, and even though I love school, I'm excited for summer and having time to play outside. The first morning, my cousins are all out in the yard, and after I dress Yasmin and Junior, we go out, too. The only thing I'm afraid of is cockle boos—I don't like the way the prickly clumps of burrs at the top of the plants stick to my clothes. We're playing tag in the yard, and Theo grabs some cockle boos and throws them at me. Some stick to his hand, but he doesn't care because most of them are stuck to me. I almost cried, but I didn't. Then Ava and Tyrone got some cockle boos and threw them at me, too. I try to duck and get away, but they just stick to me. The cockle boos poke into my skin like a lot of little needles. I hate picking them out of my clothes because touching them is gross—the tiny splinters poke me and get stuck in my palms and fingertips.

"Stop it!" I yell, but they just laugh.

"Cornbread wants us to stop." They look at each other and laugh, again. "We ain't gonna stop, Cornbread. Cause, you ain't got no mama here to make us."

My cousins call me "Cornbread" because it's my favorite food that Grandmo makes. Cornbread isn't bad, but I don't like the way they say it, taunting me by telling me I am not good. Telling me it's all of them against just me. I cry, wishing they would stop calling me names and throwing cockle boos at me. If my daddy was here, he would make them stop.

"My daddy's coming as soon as he can," I tell them. The cousins just laugh more.

"Why you talk like a white girl? Your daddy ain't coming for you, Cornbread. Your mama left you because she doesn't even like you." I stop myself from crying and I gather up Junior and Yasmin. I tell them we are good, and daddy will come for us. Those cousins don't know anything. What's wrong with the way I talk? I talk in just a normal way. Maybe it's different from them, but I don't see how. The only white people I see, really, are my teachers. They are good, and so maybe it's good if I talk like them. Those white teachers get to tell everybody else what to do. I bet they live in prettier houses, too, maybe like the big house I lived in with my daddy. That's not something I remember very much anymore, but it seems like I used to live in a place that was pretty and not always crowded and loud with people teasing me. No mean aunts, either. Maybe if I am good in school and smart, maybe my daddy will come to get us.

The good thing is that the cousins don't throw cockle boos at Junior and Yasmin. But whenever Junior and Yasmin do something that the cousins don't like, they tell their moms. Junior is playing with some old toy cars on the porch, and Maddox wants them. Junior says they can play together, but Maddox says those are his cars and Junior can't play at all. Junior grabs the cars and starts yelling, so Maddox runs into the kitchen to tell. Aunt Karen comes out.

"You're a bad boy for not sharing those cars," she says, and she snatches the cars out of his hands and gives them to Maddox. Now he's really crying, but she doesn't care. She picks Junior up and whips him. I can't stop them from whooping Junior. I can't stop any of this. At the table, when Yasmin cries because she wants something different to eat, Grandmo says this all we got so better eat or one of the aunts will slap her face. Then, I'd run over to kiss her to make her feel better, but I couldn't stop the hurting. I look at the aunt's real mean, to let them know what they do is bad. They don't care. Sometimes they say, "Get that look off your face, girl. Nobody cares what you think." Then I remember I am only kind of family because I don't have a grownup of my own here.

26

Most of the time, though, I love summer because I get to play with my brother and sister. They know that I am their family and that we love each other. Whenever I can, I hug them and hold them, even though they are getting bigger. I make up math problems because I love numbers. I teach them words and colors. I tell them they are smart, and smarter than anyone else. So, maybe when they go to school, their teachers will praise them, and they will feel happy like I do.

Chapter 5

Back to Grandmo's

"Young girls are like helpless children in the hands of amorous men, whatever is said to them is true and whatever manipulation on their bodies seems like love to them, sooner or later, they come back to their senses, but the scars are not dead inasmuch as her spoiler lives."
— Michael Bassey Johnson, Scars of Beauty

Mr. Green is principal the whole time I'm at Helmer Elementary in Jackson, Michigan. I think he must know I'm back in California with my daddy. Grandmo has already told Mr. Green my mother isn't around for me to live with her. I will be in second grade next year when school starts again, but I will be going to school in California because my Grandmo is taking us to live with daddy. I don't know who my teacher would have been or what she thinks. I am so happy and excited that I can't really think of anything else. I try to be good on the train and keep track of Yasmin and Junior because it takes a long time to get to my daddy. The train stops, again. But this time Grandmo says we are getting off. "You mean off the train", Grandmo? "She says grab your brother's hand". She is holding Yasmin. As soon as we are off the train, I see him. Tall and sharply dressed as I remember. Junior lets go of my hand and runs to him. I ran after him and to my daddy, too. We all laughed and hugged. Grandmo hands him Yasmin, but I am a big girl now. I started to think I might be going back to the way things used to be, but he says he doesn't live at our same house anymore, and *she* isn't there. When I ask, Daddy just says she is trying to become a famous singer and that I have to love her. That's okay because I have my daddy.

Daddy drives a post office truck from Los Angeles to Houston each night. We had a map of the United States on the wall at our school, and I try to picture where that is, but it's hard to remember. I just know it is far and he is gone a long time. He puts us to bed and leaves us alone at home most nights, saying, "Regina, watch your brother and sister." I am going on seven, Junior is four, and Yasmin is three. I have been taking care of them the whole time we were at Grandmo's, so it feels right that I am in charge of them here. One night I woke

28

up and Junior wasn't in bed. It's dark, and I can feel Yasmin next to me, but no Junior. I ran to the kitchen to see if he was there. We are just getting used to having enough food now that we live with Daddy, so I think maybe Junior was hungry and knew it would be okay to get up and get a snack. Yep, he got in the refrigerator, but instead of getting a snack, he is pulling stuff out of it and dropping it on the floor. I yell at him, "Daddy's going to get mad that you made a mess." He starts crying, so I hug him and tell him I'm sorry, that it's alright. I sent him back to bed. Then, I stay up to clean, picking up jars of mayonnaise, ketchup, mustard, hotdogs, and I don't know what else, and putting them back in the refrigerator as neatly as I can.

One morning, Daddy was home when we woke up. He sits me down at the kitchen table while I eat my cereal to explain to me that a lady across the street wants to babysit us. He says that she knows he has been leaving us home alone all night. I say it's okay because we sleep through most of the nights. I don't tell him about Junior getting up in the night, even though he isn't Grandmo, and I don't think he will beat Junior. He doesn't whoop us, but it's safer, I know, not to tell grownups everything.

The lady's name is Charlie just like my daddy's name. I see her coming and going from her house with a daughter who is older than me. The daughter walks funny, and Daddy says that she has something that I can't pronounce and I'm not even sure what it means. We spend the night and have to sleep on that lady, Charlie's floor in the living room. We go at night and then my dad says he will pick us up in the mornings or later when we wake up to take us back home. Daddy says he doesn't have anybody else to take care of us, and this will be better than leaving us alone.

I ask daddy, "Where is *she*? If *she* came home, *she* could take care of us."

"I don't know, but you are to always love her, you hear?"

"Yes, daddy," I tell him, and I make a promise in my heart to always love *her* no matter what.

One day we are at the babysitter's house during the day. Daddy is sleeping, so it's better if we aren't there to make so much noise. Junior and I went to the store to get candy.

M&Ms and Fritos. I am so happy that we have been given a quarter to go buy the candy that I don't even think about the last time this happened. I don't let myself because that would make me not love *her*, and I promised I would. As we left the store I started skipping back towards the babysitter's house. I am happy with my stuff.

The ground starts to shake. I get so scared. I grabbed Junior's hand, and I started running with him. The ground is still shaking as we run, so it's hard to keep my balance, and I don't want to drop my goodies or let go of Junior. I think about Yasmin and is she someplace safe? Will the ground just open up and swallow us? Why is this happening? Somehow, we make it inside the house. Charlie the lady babysitter grabs Junior and says to me, "Y'all, ok?"

"Yes," I answer, knowing worse things can happen when you go to the store to get candy. "Why is the ground shaking?"

She says, "It's an earthquake." I wonder if anywhere is safe. I cry even though I try not to.

Not long after the earthquake, Daddy sits down with me again and says, "It's hard to take care of you here, and my mother wants to take care of you." He's talking about Grandmo, but I don't like the way Grandmo, and the aunts whip us and make me do all the chores. At least I know them now. Maybe Charlie babysitter lady told him she didn't want to take care of us anymore.

"I'll be good. Junior and Yasmin will be good." I started to cry. "Daddy, why can't we stay with you? Please don't make us go," I beg. "I don't like it there. My cousins have a mom, and they tease me that mine didn't love me, so she left me." I don't tell him about all of the other things they say. I don't tell him about the whooping that Junior and Yasmin get. Grownups always think what other grownups do is right. If daddy is mad, he might send us away someplace different. That might be even worse.

"Regina, don't believe that, and remember what I said, you are to always love her."

"Where is *she*?" I ask. It's the first time I dare to speak in a hateful way.

"I don't know, but my mother loves you all very much and promised to take good care of you." He kisses me on the forehead and hugs me. The next thing I know, Grandmo is there.

As I look out the car window on the way to the train station, I think how I don't like trains anymore. They seem to be a way to leave or get left behind. Daddy puts us on the train with Grandmo. He hands Yasmin to her and lifts Junior up the stairs. I walk up the too familiar steps as I start to cry, thinking he doesn't love me either. Or why would he send me away? I turned around to give him a hug. He seems like he is about to cry too when he says good-bye.

It's another long ride, three days and three nights, to go from Northridge, California, to Jackson, Michigan. I like to look outside and see the beautiful scenery as we pass, so quiet, lots of trees, sometimes buildings, and sometimes just nothing. Fields of nothing. I lean and press my face against the window and just look. When I think about it, I ask my Grandmo why we have to go with her. She says she can take better care of us because my daddy has to work. And she owes this to him. Owes what to him? She doesn't say.

Then I ask her, "When is *she* coming back to get us?" I expect the usual answer, which had become comforting, "Baby, you gonna to be okay." Like I'm going to be okay some time. Instead, she answers, "Baby, I don't know where she is or if she is ever coming back. But I love you and will take good care of you." I know she means it, that she wants to take good care of me, and I know I will have to try to remember that through all the bad things that will probably happen again. Sometimes, I know, even grownups have bad things happen.

There's one good thing about coming back to Jackson. My cousins, Ava and Gigi, and I are excited to see each other. Even if they tease me sometimes, they are my best friends. Plus, they only are really mean when the boys are around. The boys tease everyone, but me the worst. "What you are doing back here, white girl?" they ask. And even though I know deep down that this is their way of saying I don't belong here, I pretend it's just them being silly. I can't admit what they are saying because then I will have nowhere and nobody. I try to join in and tease back, but I can never think of anything mean to tease about. Plus, I know they will tell their mamas and then I will be in trouble, just like they do with Junior, even though he's just six, and Yasmin, who is five. It's hard enough to keep them from being whipped, I don't want to get whipped, too.

Since my cousin has the same name as mine, she is called Gigi, I get to be called Jean-Jean not my real name and that's not okay with me. We only get to play for a little bit before Grandmo says, "Bedtime." Me, Junior, and Yasmin go upstairs to get in bed. My excitement about my cousins is gone because I know I'm not going to see my daddy when I wake up. I wonder what it is about me that makes the grownups I love leave me. I must deserve this, so I decided I have to be extra good, and I have to take care of Yasmin and Junior, to make sure that they don't feel sad like I do. At least they will have someone to love them. They will always have me.

I know who everyone is now. Aunt Valerie, who was born the same year as my daddy, lives far away in Washington D.C. Aunt Karen is the mean one, and Aunt Sharon is the kind one who owns a restaurant, maybe because she was closest to my dad when they were growing up. That's what's my daddy told me. Aunt Niecy lives close by, and sometimes I get to go to her house to play with Gabrielle. Aunt Danielle is hardly around, but she sends her kids over every day. She isn't too mean, but she isn't very nice, either. Maybe because she really doesn't talk to us. My Aunt Karen whips Yasmin and Junior all the time. All it takes is one of her kids saying Yasmin or Junior called them names or hit one of them, whether it's the truth or a lie. It makes me sad, and I try to protect Junior and Yasmin by playing with them outside and keeping them away from trouble. I don't want to get whipped, so I make sure to be on my best behavior all the time, just like Mrs. Schiklen says at school. If anyone yells at me, I just cry, so they never bother to whip me, too. Plus, if they send us away, I don't know where we will have to go.

One night, Junior and Yasmin are staying the night at Aunt Niecy's. The other Regina or Gigi is on one of her visits with her dad, and Ava and her brother Theo are with their mom. Grandpa is off drinking. I don't feel good, so I say I want to stay home, alone. The house that is usually so full of people and noise is quiet, so I fall asleep, and Grandmo leaves me to myself. My two oldest boy cousins climb into the bed with me and wake me up. One on each side of me. I am quiet, not sure what they are doing there and what I should do. They hardly ever pay me any attention other than teasing, so I wonder if this is a game, and they are letting me in because I'm the only other kid here. I wait to see what happens. I had learned in the closet, and during the kissing game with Uncle Tommy, that I am supposed to be quiet no matter what. I stay quiet when Maddox, the smaller cousin who was just nine years old, raises up my nightgown and spreads my legs apart, then climbs on top of me. He starts pumping up and down on me.

"Get off me. Please stop," I cry. I don't have to be quiet for this. It's hard to breathe and he is pushing down really hard on my privates through my underwear. It doesn't really hurt between my legs, but mostly it's just scary, this feeling that they can do whatever they want because they are bigger and stronger. If the kissing game with Uncle Tommy is wrong, the pumping game must be wrong, too.

Maddox doesn't listen to me and keeps going until the older cousin says, "It's my turn." Maddox listens to Tyrone and gets off of me so the really big and fat twelve-year-old can start his turn. "You are hurting me, stop!" I say through muffled tears, "I'm going to tell Grandmo." Grandmo is downstairs but every time I try to call out to her Maddox puts his hand over my mouth and tells me to shut up.

Instead of stopping, Tyrone pulls out his private part and begins pumping me up and down for what seems like forever. I try to pretend it isn't me lying there, getting crushed by this big cousin with his stinky breath and stupid grin. It's hard to breathe, but I catch my breath whenever I can with my eyes closed wishing for him to stop, to leave me alone. Wishing I was where I was supposed to be, not in this terrible house with people who are supposed to be my family. My family is *her* and Daddy and Junior and Yasmin and even Kim.

I don't know if I am allowed to fight. I don't know if fighting will do me any good. They are bigger and stronger, and I am not really part of the family, not for real. I want to go back to California, to my dad, to nowhere, to anywhere. Why would anyone worry about me?

In bed in the middle of the two boys, I am crying, and my body and my feelings hurt. Maddox says, "It's my turn again. I didn't get to do it that way."

Tyrone yells, "Wait a minute." Then, I feel the wetness on my leg, and the heavy one gets off me. I let out a breath, thinking it's over. The smaller one takes another turn. No wetness when he finally climbs off me. They both warn that I better not tell anyone, or they will do it again. I know what they did is wrong, that what they did isn't something that should be done to me. But I am scared. They leave me alone and I wipe my thigh with the bed cover before turning over to cry. Where is *she* or my Daddy?

One day, something good happens. A lady called Ellie Mae comes to visit. She has presents for me, Junior, and Yasmin. She says my daddy sent her to see us and gave us these new clothes. I tear open the wrapping paper and there is a beautiful dress. It's brown with flowers, and Yasmin has one to match. Junior has boys' clothes. Grandmo tells Ellie Mae that she can take us into her bedroom to try on the dresses. We are never allowed in Grandmo's room, so this is exciting. Plus, we never get new clothes. The clothes I wear are mostly hand-me-downs from cousins, but I am the skinniest person in the house, so a lot of the clothes don't really fit me. Sometimes I'm called "Skinny bones." But in the brown dress, I feel beautiful. I can't wait to wear it to church.

Going to Grandmo's church is one of the best parts of my week, except school. All the ladies say how cute I look, and what long hair I have, and everybody is nice. I love to sing the songs, and I don't even mind sitting still while the pastor talks. After church, the whole family comes over to Grandmo's for Sunday dinner. We have always had collard greens which are my favorite next to cornbread and candied yams. Sometimes fried chicken or fish we caught. Grandmo cooks most Saturday night to be ready, and I get to help. There are so many people, and all of the food is gobbled up, but I always get something to eat, at least on Sundays.

Chapter 6

The Whipping Pole

"Some days you'll hold the sorrow between your teeth and smile tightly to keep it from escaping." — Minerva Jean, For the Secrets That Gave Themselves Away

On the first day of school, Grandmo takes me and Junior to Helmer Elementary. He's the one in kindergarten now. As we walked into the building, I held his hand and told him he was going to have fun at school. That he will be playing, but he has to remember the things I taught him, like how to count and his colors, too. On the train I taught him to count to a hundred.

I'm in the second grade still, just like I was in California. Already I can barely remember school there. I'm seven years old for the second part of the school year, big enough to take care of myself and my sister and brother. My teacher is the same teacher I had for first grade, Miss Robertson. I come up to her shoulders. She is white—but I think all teachers must be white—with reddish curly hair and freckles on her face, like Yasmin. Even though all the teachers are white, there aren't a lot of white kids. In Simi Valley all the kids were white, except me and Tina Davis. In the school I just went to in California, the kids were all different. At Helmer, all the kids look like me and my cousins.

Miss Schiklen always smiles. I don't feel strange around her, even on the first day. I hug her when I come into school, and she hugs me back—and I think it's just like in first grade and she will hug me every day. I love her. Miss Schiklen makes a big smile when she says hi, taking my hand from Grandmo's. I don't mind when Grandmo leaves me to go to work. School is a happy place for me, and I like to be there. I can't be with daddy, and *she* might never come back, but the adults at school are always nice to me. I love doing schoolwork. I love learning. When Ms. Schiklen shows me to my desk, I ask, "Do I share my desk?"

"No, Regina, this is your very own desk. You sit in it every day you come to school." I smile my biggest smile, and she smiles back. I think I will like second grade, but the lessons are so easy. I always get done before the other kids and have to sit at my desk, bored. I already learned some of my multiplications in California. I can't wait to go out on the playground and play with my cousins. It's better than playing at Grandmo's house.

In second grade, I learned how to read a clock with Roman numerals. That is so fun. (*It's a pleasant memory as an adult. I bought my own Roman numeral clocks, and it makes me smile thinking about the little girl I was, so excited to learn*). When I do multiplication, I am amazed at how the numbers work together and just make sense. I like the way everything has a time and a place, math before recess, story time after lunch. I like learning new things and when the teacher smiles at me. "You're such a smart girl. Good work." It's the truth and that I will do almost anything to hear those words. At Grandmo's house, no matter how hard I work, there is always more work to do. There are so many people, and no grownup is my grownup. With all the noise and fighting, I am most likely to get name calling. Whenever I do anything to show I am good or smart, my cousins tease me for being a white girl. If I could, I would stay at school all day.

Two of my cousins go to school with me and one cousin, Gabrielle, goes to a different elementary school but is in my same grade. The four of us were all born in the same year, 1963. I like having them at school with me, especially on the playground, even though they tease me about sounding white, just like all the other kids at school. I know sounding white is bad, but I don't know how to change how I talk. I just think about how my teachers think I'm smart when the kids tease me. It makes it a little better. And on the playground, I make sure I show the other kids who's boss. I can do more flips than anybody on the bar, so they stop teasing me about how I talk. It's like my daddy says, *people respect you when you do something better than they can.* I wish I could make it happen all the time, but it's not something I'm in charge of.

Every morning, I looked forward to going to school. I have to hold Junior's hand the whole six blocks--and I am skipping, so he has to run or skip, too. We get to play with my cousins in the playground before the bell rings. When the bell

36

rings, I grab Junior's hand and take him to his classroom, on the first floor, just like mine.

I love the monkey bars and merry-go-round. This girl named Paula plays on the monkey bars with me. Paula is my first friend in Jackson besides my cousins. So is another boy called Peter. When I am at school, playing with my cousins and my friends or learning new things in my class, I am so happy. It is easy to forget, for just a little while, that *she* left us and that I will go back to Grandmo's and have to do work.

I can tell Mrs. Schiklen is happy with me because I answer her questions, and she looks at me in a smiling way. She says I am so far ahead of the other kids in class and tells me she wants to talk to my parents. Since my parents aren't there, she sends a note home for Grandmo.

Grandmo and I sit at the table in Mrs. Schiklen's room after school. It feels weird to have my two different worlds in the same place. I try to sit quietly with my hands folded in my lap like I'm supposed to show them both that I am a good girl. It's hard to sit still because I am trying hard to listen and understand what the grownups are saying about me. Miss Schiklen tells Grandmo that I am ahead of the other kids and because of this she would like me to skip the third grade and go on to the fourth grade. I hear Grandmo immediately say no. Miss Schiklen tries to explain how important it is to my education to make sure I am learning new things. I feel so proud of myself, which I know I shouldn't, but it is so wonderful when an adult is saying good things about me. My grandmother continues to say she doesn't want me to be ahead of my cousins. Grandmo decides, and I do what she says. I am going to third grade.

I don't suck my thumb when I am in school, but I do when I am at home. It's comforting, and Yasmin and Junior do it, too. When Grandmo or one of the aunts sees us, they tell us to stop. I can remember to stop for a while, but then, when I'm feeling sad, I put my thumb back in my mouth. And now I'm sad about not skipping the third grade. Grandmo yells, "Take your hand out of your mouth." Aunt Sharon tells us nicely. Aunt Karen says, "I'm going to get the hot sauce." Aunt Karen puts the hot sauce on all of our thumbs, and it dries on. I forget, and I put my thumb back in my mouth. It burns. A lot. I tried to get a glass of water, but it didn't help. The burning keeps going. I know I will hate hot sauce all my life. Every time I put my thumb in my mouth, Aunt Karen gets out the hot sauce. I know I might forget and do it again, and I know it will burn. I just can't stop. My cousins don't do it, but they don't tease me about it, which is one good thing because we are together all the time.

The summer comes and goes so fast. Nothing to remember to tell the other classmates about my summer. I did enjoy teaching my brother and sister more letters and adding up numbers. That's my favorite part of summer when I don't have to go fishing. I usually can't wait to go back to school but since I am not skipping a grade, I wonder what it will be like.

In third grade, something changed. I no longer ask when Daddy is coming to take me home because I know this is where I live now. School is different, too. My new teacher, Miss Boatman, who is tall and chubby with brown and blonde hair and glasses, is not as friendly as my other teachers were. She doesn't smile, not at me, and not at the other kids, and she doesn't seem excited when we are learning something new. I'm just bored. I start to hate school, and I don't feel like being smart is a good thing anymore. Kids get mad at me for raising my hand to answer questions all the time. They say you already know the answer. Miss Boatman tries to quiet me. She says I can't talk when I'm done with work. I can't do more work or read. I just have to sit in my place. I stare out the window and wish I could be outside. If school isn't my special place, and home isn't my special place, at least I have the monkey bars. I am now the kid who only waits for recess.

The only thing I really like about third grade is that we have spelling bees in our class to review vocabulary words. I know a lot of words because I love to read. I always get the word right. Miss Boatman doesn't seem happy when I raise my hand, but I'm not sure why. Teachers are supposed to like it when kids are smart. Maybe the other kids don't like it, but if I know the words and they don't, why shouldn't I win the spelling bee? Miss Boatman pulls me aside on the way out to recess one day and tells me that we are having a spelling bee after we get back, and I am not allowed to raise my hand. I feel like my heart has fallen and tears are jumping to my eyes, but I fight them back. I am shocked at the feeling of rejection.

Whatever happens in the rest of my life, I never expected to feel this way at school.

I decided that third grade is bad, and I don't care about it anymore. I spent the rest of the school year afraid to say anything. Most of the time I am sad and bored. The rest of the class is learning math and English and all the things you are supposed to learn in third grade, but I just finish my work as fast as I can and stare out the window.

I still like recess and lunch. On the playground, Peter ran up to me and kissed me. I thought this is ok, right? I thought if he does it again, I'd better have stopped sucking my thumb. All of the hot sauce and yelling at home didn't change this, but somehow, I knew since a boy said he liked me, I was too big to suck my thumb. But he never kissed me again, probably because the teacher saw him and said don't touch that girl again.

Lunch is in the gym. We walk from the classroom to the gym in straight lines every afternoon. Boys in one line, girls in the other. I usually bring my lunch, but sometimes there isn't anything to pack, so I just try to make it, so nobody notices. If I'm lucky, a friend will have some extra food, and I will get a few bites. One day, Miss Boatman sees I don't have a lunch bag. She says I should walk home for lunch. Lots of kids live in walking distance and go home during lunch hour, sometimes to get something to eat, or watch tv, or sometimes because they have to help out at home. I know there is no food and no tv if I go home, plus I would miss lunchtime recess, which is the most fun recess. Miss Boatman insists I can't stay at school all day with no food. I tell her there won't be food at home for me to eat anyway. Grandmo, I think, is at work, so only Aunt Karen will be there to feed us lunch. I'm tired of walking home for Aunt Karen to say there isn't anything for me to eat. Miss Boatman thinks I am just being sassy, tells me I have had an attitude since she talked to me about my behavior during spelling bees. I have no choice but to walk home.

I really don't want to go to Grandmo's, so I stopped at Aunt Sharon's restaurant on the way home. As soon as I walk in the door, Aunt Sharon is on me. She says, "Jean-Jean you are in big trouble. You ran your mouth off at that school lying saying that you didn't have enough food to eat." My stomach begins to knot as fright sets in. Aunt Sharon says that my teacher called Grandmo, and Grandmo called her, looking for me. Aunt Sharon isn't about to go against Grandmo. She says I embarrassed the family and sends me home without giving me anything to eat. I walk the next two blocks to my Grandmo's house, trembling. I've seen Grandmo get mad plenty of times and I know what is waiting for me.

When I get there Grandmo says, "Take off your clothes down to your slip." She makes me hug the pole that supports the wall between the bedroom and living room. I'm shaking and crying, telling her I'm sorry. I didn't mean it. She ignores my pleas and ties my hands together around the pole. I feel like I might fall over if I wasn't tied to the pole. Grandmo walks away and when she comes back, she has a long extension cord that she uses to whip me. She is in a fury. I scream at every lash. Each time she strikes, she repeats that I am never to talk about what happens in her house to anybody. Finally, when I begin to bleed through my slip from the welts that are forming on my body, she tells me to go upstairs. I am in such terrible pain, but all I can think about is her saying with every lash to never talk outside this house.

As I walk up the stairs, taking one at a time, trying not to jiggle and make the pain on my stinging back worse, I hear her yell, "And don't you dare tell anyone what happened here today." I know Grandmo is sometimes mean and angry, but I have always been careful not to make her mad. Over the years, I had seen my sister and brother get whipped, a lot of the time for little things, but I had never seen anything as brutal as the whooping I just had. I don't know why she is so angry. Does she think I lied when I told the teacher? Or does she know what I said is the truth, and does she feel ashamed? There were always so many people at Grandmo's, and they all ate before me and Junior and Yasmin. When I pack lunches, I make sure Junior has food first, and sometime, too many times, I don't have anything left for me. Even though I help my grandma pick the grapes from her backyard vines, apples off the apple tree, and collard greens and turnips out of the ground, I am always the last one to get to eat. Grandmo grows a lot in her backyard, but with that and groceries, there just isn't enough food. When I pick and clean the food from Grandmo's garden, I usually feel jealous that my cousins can just go into the backyard and play without having to work. When they get to eat the food and

40

I don't, that's even worse. But I don't say anything. I'd learn to be quiet. I learn not to tell. Until today.

Me, my sister, and cousins are outside playing in Grandmo's side yard when my cousin Theo, Ava's brother, who is six, just a year older than Yasmin, picks up a brick and throws it at my sister. Immediately, my sister screams, and I screams as soon as I see all the blood running down her head. We are used to being picked on because we don't have a parent there to make sure nobody messes with us, but this is too much. Yasmin is bleeding so much that I'm getting scared. All the cousins act like they don't know what happened or where that brick came from. I tried to pick up Yasmin, but she is screaming and bleeding and won't stay still. Blood is getting all over me, and Junior is there crying, too, now. I wonder if we are going to get in trouble.

My Aunt Sharon hears the commotion and calls us inside. Aunt Sharon wipes off the blood and tells Yasmin to lay down and she will be alright. I don't think she will be alright, and I am mad. Theo will for sure get away with this. His mom, Karen, isn't there, but she would most likely yell at me or Yasmin for this, not Theo. Nobody is going to stand up for us. I've never done anything bad while we were staying at Grandmo's and I don't want another whooping, but I feel so angry that I want to scream, "Yasmin's not okay, and it matters what happens to us." It matters what happens to me. I don't scream and I don't know if anyone would do anything but slap my mouth for sassing if I did. I storm outside with my fists balled up, and there is Theo, playing with the cousins as if nothing had just happened. So, I hit him. And this might be the one time I get away with something. Nobody could say he didn't deserve it.

Yasmin is sent to bed. After I change out of my bloody clothes, I go to check on her, to wake her up because it is time for her favorite cartoon to come on. Probably nobody else will check on her. She comes downstairs with me, and we sit in front of the television to watch *Spiderman*. Right away she falls back and starts shaking. I can see her eyes rolling back in her head. It's scarier than the blood running down the front of her face earlier. I scream.

My Aunt Sharon, who is sitting in the kitchen, comes over to her and tries to help by sitting her up but Yasmin slumps back down again. My aunt yells for someone to get her a spoon. I'm crying and scared but I got her a spoon and brought it back. The other kids are just standing in the doorway, behind Yasmin and Aunt Sharon. No one says a single word--it's that scary. Aunt Sharon takes the spoon and puts it in my sister's mouth. I don't know what that is supposed to do, and I wish for somebody to do something to help Yasmin for real. Finally, there is no other choice, and someone calls an ambulance.

The sirens are loud as the ambulance pulls up to our driveway. The living room fills up with white men in white clothes. They put my sister on a bed and took her away. I cry and say I want to go with her, but nobody is really paying attention to me other than to say get out of the way. I say, "She's only five. She needs me." I'm afraid the white men will take her away and she won't be able to come back. Days and days pass, and Yasmin doesn't come home. We aren't allowed to go see her. Will she think that Junior and I didn't want her? When I asked my aunt who had put the spoon in her mouth, she told me that the doctors couldn't do anything for her here at the hospital in Jackson and that she had to be taken to the University of Michigan hospital in Ann Arbor. They say with sadness in her voice, so I know it is someplace important, which means probably something bad is happening.

I'm not asking when *she* is coming to get us anymore, but now every day I ask my aunts and Grandmo when Yasmin is coming home. They say they ain't sure. I go to bed crying because my sister is somewhere, and I can't be with her. I know she needs me. She's hurt and scared and surrounded by grownups she doesn't know. I've seen what it's like in hospitals on tv shows, so I know there's nothing good happening there. And I can't even give her a hug the way I do when Aunt Karen whoops her or the cousins tease her. I can't help her go to sleep. I just hope she comes home.

Then the day comes. Grandmo comes into the house with my sister. I am so happy when she runs to me, and she hugs me. She knows I didn't want to leave her. I hugged her so tight, and I held onto her like I will never let her go. Junior comes over and hugs us, too. We are a little circle with all the others on the outside. It is my job to keep us like that no matter what.

Whenever I'm on the phone with Daddy, Grandmo and my aunts stand over me while I talk. Daddy calls right after Yasmin got hurt. They all tell me not to tell Daddy about my sister. Nobody says the word *hurt* or *blood*. They seem afraid, but I just think it's because they feel bad, they haven't been taking care of us good enough. But a few days later, he called again, and I let myself forget about their warnings and I told him. Right away, I can hear anger in his voice. He says he needs to talk to Grandmo, so I handed her the phone. My aunts hear everything, and I can see the scared looks on their faces. After Grandmo hangs up, the house goes crazy and the aunts all start yelling at me saying I should have kept my big mouth shut. They are yelling at me that now there will be trouble when my daddy comes back. They keep saying my daddy will be angry enough to come to Jackson to make them pay. I don't understand that; I just want him to come and take us away so we can live with him again. Daddy is the only one who never whooped us or yelled at us. I want Yasmin and Junior and me to be safe.

Then one night, I felt a hand on my shoulder, my daddy woke me up just a little while after I went to bed. It's dark so I think I'm dreaming. My daddy is here! No way. Yasmin and Junior are still sleeping, so it's just the two of us. When we go downstairs nobody is there. It looks like my aunts and uncles have scattered. The ones who live with Grandmo have gone someplace else, and the ones who don't must have just stayed away that night. Uncle Tommy is the most scared of my dad and seems to have just disappeared. Aunt Danielle's kids aren't even there, and they usually get to stay up way past my bedtime. I start to wonder if this is why everybody has been acting so strange all week. They have all been mad at me, but everybody avoids saying anything or even mentioning my dad's name.

I am so happy to see him, that's all I can think about. I can't resist asking him where *she* is, but he says he doesn't know. It isn't real hope that makes me ask; I just have always asked so I do it now. He says I have to love her. I wonder why

I have to keep loving her if she doesn't love me. I try to feel love for her, and somewhere deep down, I hope she will come back, but I can't even imagine what that will be like. I feel like my dad loves me enough to come back, even if he sent us away. *She* doesn't come back, which means she doesn't love us. I know that I have to love, even if I don't deserve to be loved.

We sit in the living room and talk. Daddy asks me questions about how I have been. Grandmo is standing somewhere between the dining room and living room, being nosy, but I'm not afraid of her when my daddy is here. I tell him about the work I have to do and the way I am hungry sometimes because I have to make sure Yasmin and Junior have food. He gets more and more upset that we were not taken care of like he thought. He says, "I sent her money all the time. You guys should not want for anything."

We sit together for a while and Daddy hugs me and says he has to go. I cry because I think he is leaving us again. But he gets up anyway and talks to Grandmo. They seem to be in an argument. Nobody can argue with Daddy except Grandmo. I heard him say that he is going to find Karen and Tommy. Karen is Theo's mom, and he's the one who had thrown the brick at my sister. I don't know why he wants Tommy. I could see Daddy had a gun in his back side. I heard him say he will use it if he has to. I know his serious voice.

Chapter 7

Daddy's Home

"I used to think that what scared me was the idea of being abandoned until someone said to me, 'Only children can be abandoned. Adults can't be abandoned because we have a choice. Children don't have a choice. '" —Demi Moore

We moved in with Frankie Mae and her two kids, a daughter named Susan who is six months older than me, and a son named Odin roughly three months older than my brother. I think Frankie Mae looks like a church lady—a big body with a small head like those women who sing really loud in church. She isn't like my mom or other women I saw my dad with. She lives in a duplex townhouse, *later I learned this was the Projects.* I get to go to the same school. I'm glad. Helmer Elementary is the one thing I can count on no matter where I live in Jackson, and I am finishing third grade. I don't like school so much this year, but I love being at home with my own family. My daddy is gone a lot of the time. But I don't really know what a normal amount of time for a daddy to be home, so I guess the way we are living is right. I stop asking about *her*. I am eight and it has been three years since *she* left us. I have a new family now.

Susan, Odin, Junior and I all walk to school together and we walk home together, too. The good part of third grade is playing on the playground and having a big sister. Susan is in the same grade because she was held back because of her asthma. We get to play together. One day when we were walking home, Daddy and Frankie Mae pulled up alongside us in Daddy's white Cadillac. Frankie Mae gets out of the car to show us a diamond ring. It looks skinny and little to me, but she seems really happy about it. Susan and I are excited because we know what this means. They are married. We hugged each other and jumped up and down. "My daddy and your mommy will be together forever. We are sisters for real."

We settled into a regular life, just like a family, just like I wanted. I think that I finally have someone I can call *mama*. Frankie Mae stays home to take care of us and Daddy leaves when he works, and he isn't even home much at night. But on weekends, everybody is home, and us kids play in the backyard open to all the project homes.

Daddy makes sure we know that we are all a family. One time, Mama Baxter sent me, Junior, and Yasmin five dollars each. We are so happy when we open the envelope, and we each take our five-dollar bill and dance around, talking about all of the great things we will buy. My dad takes out his wallet and gives Susan and Odin five dollars. He says, "You don't treat the kids in your family different." He tells us to never use the word *step*. I know we are all a family, and I am starting to feel safe and comfortable.

The address on the envelope is the same one that Mama Baxter told me to remember. I don't know how she knows our address. Mama Baxter is the lady *she* took us to see before dropping us off at Grandmo's. It seems like such a long time ago that I'm not sure anymore if it even really happened. I asked daddy about her, and he says that she is my grandmother and that she has my sister Veronica. He explains that Mama Baxter has a lot to take care of. Even if we don't get to see her, it is nice that she sent us a gift.

Daddy doesn't celebrate birthdays or Christmas, but going on vacation is huge for him. To him, vacation means going to see family. For black parents, that's what vacation means for most everyone. Unless you're rich, then you might go to Disneyworld or something, but nobody I know does anything like the white people do on TV. One day he announces that he wants to take all of us with Frankie Mae to see her brother in Buffalo. To get there, he says, you have to go through Detroit, so we can go to see his grandmother, the one who raised him when he was a teenager after his stepfather kicked him out in Chattanooga.

"Y'all get your stuff and get in the car." We have only a few minutes to pile into the car, and all five of us kids get into the back seat of his white Cadillac. Daddy turns on the music and I drift away loving the sound of music. One of the best things about riding in my dad's car was the music. Dad played us music at home—he loves Curtis Blo—but the music I heard on the radio wasn't the same. We rarely heard black songs on the radio. (*On the trip to Buffalo, I heard the Beatles,*

Rod Stewart, and Led Zeppelin. My favorite was a song called 'Cats in the Cradle'. Don't know why, but I'd never forgot it. I also learned to love country music. My dad actually liked country music and even wore cowboy hats). There are mainly white people songs on the radio, but I like them almost as much as the music my daddy plays on his record player at home.

We pull up to a house that daddy says is his grandma's house. We meet an old woman who is almost the same height as me. Her name is Fannie, but we are to call her Big Ma, and I can tell my dad loves her so much. I think she's scary, but when she hugs me, I hug her back. Her hair is straight and very black, and it hangs almost to her knees. It tickles my face when she pulls me close to her. Daddy is so happy and excited to see her. He says our names to her. Yasmin and Junior huddled close to Daddy. I think they're scared, too. We don't stay too long, though, and we are back in the car listening to music again.

While we are in Detroit, Daddy wants to show us our three other sisters and their mom. We stopped at their house and met a lady named Rachel. The girls' names are Georgia who is the oldest and was named after his brother George, who didn't live with Grandmo. The second girl is Patricia Anne, and the baby is Sharon Anne. She has the same name as Aunt Sharon. Sharon Anne is just two years older than me.

"These are your sisters," Daddy tells us. We hug. They seem happy to meet me. They kind of look like me. Or I look like them. Being in their house is a weird feeling. I feel jealous that they have their real mom to live with them. Daddy seems to have had a lot of wives, and he seems to go from one to the next. Rachel has Daddy's real kids, so they are our real family. Still, I'm glad he doesn't ask us to call her *mama*, too.

Before it gets too late, we have to go so we can make it to Buffalo, New York, to see Frankie Mae's brother. Once again, we are in the car, listening to music. It's nighttime and dark outside, and the whole world seems to only matter inside the car. Until we drive further.

Daddy tells us that there is a bridge and a tunnel to get into Canada. We are going to take the tunnel on the way there, and the bridge on the way back. Daddy makes it sound like a magical adventure, just like in my books. Everybody in the car is excited. The tunnel goes on for miles. It is a little scary, but

Daddy is driving, so I know it will be okay. There are lights all along the tunnel and when cars pass us on the other side, their headlights blink into our eyes. When we drive out of the tunnel, I squinch up my eyes because the light is suddenly so bright.

I'm too eager to see everything to sleep much during the drive. Plus, I love reading the signs on the big billboards. I also love to count the white numbers on the green signs that sometimes go up and sometimes go down as we drive. It's okay to meet Frankie Mae's brother, but he isn't really my family, and I keep wishing I could have stayed longer to play with my sisters in Detroit. We don't get to stop there on the way home. We do get to ride over the bridge. I am absolutely amazed by the feeling of floating over the water with the sky right outside my window. I ask Daddy why there is a bridge and a tunnel on the road, and he says it is how we connect two countries, the USA and Canada. I can't believe that I have gone to another country. I remember Ms. Schiklen showed us on the globe, the country above Michigan is Canada.

Chapter 8

He Don't Miss

"All I know is, the violence rose from the fear like smoke from a fire, and I cannot say whether that violence, even administered in fear and love, sounded the alarm or choked us at the exit." –Ta-Naheisi Coates, *Between the World and Me*

We've only been living with Frankie Mae for a few months. When my daddy is home, he is fun and loving. But sometimes he seems scary, mostly when he drinks whiskey from that bottle he has. Nights are quiet time and Daddy, and I sit together to watch his favorite shows, *Bonanza* and *Gunsmoke*. Daddy loves John Wayne. He gets really excited when there is a gunfight. He says, "John Wayne really knows how to use a gun. He doesn't miss."

One night I'm sitting on a chair, about ten feet across from Daddy. He's scrunched down in the corner between the sofa and a wall. Probably, like he's still an army man in the Korean war. Frankie Mae, Susan, Odin, and Junior are sitting on that couch. My dad has rested his sawed-off shotgun across the arm of the couch, and it's pointed at me.

He says, "Regina, I want you to get up and run around the corner. See if I miss." I immediately say, "No daddy." I'm too scared to move. I know why my Grandmo was scared of my daddy with a gun. He is really scary. He says again, "Get up, just get up and run around the corner and see if I can shoot you." My dad told me about the army when he was a sharpshooter. He's like John Wayne. He doesn't miss. I am pretty scared because somehow, I know my daddy will fire that rifle.

He says a third time, "Regina, get up and run around the corner, see if you can beat me." Frankie Mae pleads with him not to play this game. He says shut up. Everyone else is quiet. With one hand on the rifle and the other waving me to get up and run he says, "I will shoot, but you might be faster." I begin to cry uncontrollably. He keeps daring me to run. Frankie May keeps pleading with him to put the gun away. Somehow, he gets tired of the game and lowers his rifle. I am so scared that I pee my pants, so I finally run, this time I go upstairs to my room I share with Susan and Yasmin to change clothes. Yasmin is in there asleep.

I stay with her, and nobody comes up to help me. They just stay downstairs watching tv, I guess. My heart is thumping and my hands tremble. I can't stop crying, even if it might wake up Yasmin. I kind of want to wake up Yasmin so somebody will hug me. This was worse even than watching *her* leave me in a cab or having Grandmo whoop me. It's worse than anything my cousins or uncle did while I lived there. All I could think was '*I was going to die'*. And it was my daddy, who was supposed to save and protect me. I wonder why daddy acted like those guys in *Gunsmoke*. It is starting to seem like no place is safe.

My daddy drinks a lot every weekend. And when he drinks, he gets out his guns. He talks about being in the army and killing people, and he seems excited about it, but he doesn't say he is going to shoot one of us again. Not for a while. One weekend Daddy and Frankie Mae have company to play cards. It's a couple who lived in a building behind us. The kids stay in the living room watching tv while they play cards at the kitchen table. But we want to know what the grownups are saying so my brother and I sneak and sit on the stairs between the living room and kitchen where we can hear, me at the top and Junior just below me. The lady keeps putting her hand on Frankie Mae's thigh. I know that because daddy keeps telling her to stop. He sounds mad.

Finally, daddy says, "You put your hand on my wife again, I'm going to shoot your hand off, bull dagger." I am scared because I know he means it. He is drinking, so I know he has one of his guns with him. Then we heard a gunshot. I ran upstairs but could still hear all the yelling downstairs. Junior stays on the stairs. There is so much screaming and commotion that I'm not sure what is happening. Daddy shot at that lady's hand, and even though he didn't kill her, it's bad. Daddy tells Junior, "I'm going to go to jail. You take care of your sisters." Junior is just six. The police came, and I know I won't see Daddy for a long time.

At first, our days are the same even though Daddy isn't there. I am happy when I go to school, but when I come home, I'm sad again because now Daddy has left us, just like *her.*

Susan and I play outside, and that is kind of fun. But Frankie Mae seems like she is going crazy. She is huge and her hair is cut off and she smells because she never takes a bath. Frankie Mae smokes cigarettes all the time.

If Frankie Mae catches me before I go outside, she makes me do weird things. Like she makes a fire in an ashtray and has me stare into the fire and imagine the future. Why did she pick me? Maybe I can predict the future. I try really hard, but mostly I just remember the past. I don't like it because those memories aren't happy. I make up stuff that I think she will want to hear because I want to get away from her smelly breath. I tell her Daddy will be home soon and we will be happy. I wish with all my heart that this is true.

Frankie Mae tells us she has to go on welfare because she doesn't have enough money without my daddy. She sends Junior and Odin to go outside to search on the sidewalks for money people dropped. They aren't allowed to come home until they get some money, so even though they are just six and seven they had to find some way to get a little cash, even if it means asking strangers. Some nights they don't come back until really late. I stay up worrying, but Frankie Mae only cares about how much money they get. One time they didn't come back all night. Frankie Mae keeps me home to look into the fire. Susan has asthma and Yasmin is too young, so she leaves them alone.

Sometimes Frankie Mae is nice, and we can use our money for candy at Top Notch, the neighborhood store. One time, a white lady follows Junior and me into the store. She tells us that my daddy told her to come and get us. She wants us to follow her out of the store and get into the car. I don't know this lady. I can't go with her; even if Junior is with me, we can't leave Yasmin. Plus, my daddy never told me about any white lady. She could be anybody. Junior and I didn't get our candy, we just rushed home to tell Frankie Mae. If she is angry or upset, I don't know it. We aren't allowed to go to the Top-Notch store anymore.

Frankie Mae tells me and Susan that we have to learn about being a woman, about being on the rag. She has been more upset and weirder lately. She has us follow her into the utility room next to the kitchen and says this is what we will have to do when we are on the rag. She pulls down her pants and pulls a rag out of her underwear. Then she relieves herself in the big mop bucket. She tells us to look in the bucket so we can see. There's blood in the bucket and on the rag, and I get scared. Has she been shot? Is she going to die? She rinses the rag out in the sink and a stream of pink water flows from it. I am freaking out. Why is this happening? Why is she showing us? I never want to be a woman and be on the rag. I want to get back to playing so I can get out of here.

Some days my Aunt Karen comes over. Frankie Mae doesn't let her in the house, even though they were friends before, and Daddy said Aunt Karen is the one who introduced him to Frankie Mae. I can hear Aunt Karen asking Frankie Mae if she can take us kids to visit Grandmo for the day. Frankie Mae says no. Aunt Karen comes again on another day, but Frankie Mae doesn't let us go. I don't know if I want to go to Grandmo's house, but I would like to see my cousins. It's summer vacation, so it's not like at school when I used to get to see my cousins on the playground. Whenever Aunt Karen comes, Frankie Mae keeps her outside and we aren't allowed to see her. It feels like Frankie Mae is getting weirder.

Chapter 9

Things Fall Apart

**"Forgiveness doesn't excuse their actions.
Forgiveness stops their actions from destroying your
heart." —Karen Salmansohn, author**

One day, a police officer knocks at the door. Frankie
Mae answers the door. She can't keep the police out like she
did with Aunt Karen. Yasmin and I are in the living room
playing when the police officer announces, "I am here to take
the Moore children." Why is a policeman coming to get us? It's
just Yasmin and me here. Will we have to leave Junior?

I say, "Junior's not here."

He just looks at me and says, "You and your sister
have to come with me now."

He holds my hand while picking my sister up and we
walk across the street to the car with lights on top. The lights
are blinking, and the neighbors have come out to watch. I am
so afraid, I want to cry, but I have to be sure we don't leave
Junior behind. I tremble when I tell the officer that Junior is
probably playing somewhere in the neighborhood. We can
drive around to find him, but I think Junior will also be afraid if
he sees a police car with its lights blinking coming after him.
There is nothing I can do. The officer puts us in the back of his
squad car. It feels like a nightmare that can't be real as we
drive around the projects in Jackson looking for my brother.
We find him on the other side of the projects walking with
Odin. The police officer tells Odin to go home and puts my
brother in the car with us. So now I'm looking at my little
brother and sister in the back of a police car not understanding
what is happening to us.

I start to recognize the neighborhood outside the car
window. We take the same roads we take when we go to the
store. Then he keeps going. He is taking us to Grandmo's
house. I'm finally able to breathe, and I tell Junior and Yasmin
that we are going to be okay. They look so scared and little in
the big backseat. But I feel relieved. I think we are going to be
okay. I'm not going to have to do any of the crazy things
Frankie Mae wanted me to do, like stare into an ashtray or

watch her pee in a bucket. At least Junior won't have to go out on the streets for money anymore. Grandmo's house is not so bad, and at least we'll be with our family. And maybe we'll be able to see daddy, and nobody will hurt Junior and Yasmin because daddy is here. I don't even care if I have to go fishing or do chores. At least Grandmo loves us, that's what daddy said. She will take care of us better than Frankie Mae.

Grandmo puts all three of us back in the upstairs bedroom where we stayed before. It's across the hall from Aunt Karen's room. Our room used to be her kids' room, but now they have to stay with her. We stay in there playing most of the time, but we are only there a few days. We are sitting on the bed playing when smoke starts coming in the room. It's a big gray cloud, and everything is fuzzy. Junior and Yasmin start coughing. I gathered both of them and ran down the stairs. We are coughing and making a commotion, so Grandmo comes out of the kitchen asking what's going on. I tell her, "Fire upstairs. Aunt Karen's room." She runs upstairs and comes back to call the fire department. When they gets there, the firefighter talks to Karen and Grandmo. He says that the fire was started on purpose. Did Aunt Karen start it? Why would she do start a fire? After the firemen leaves, Grandmo yells at Karen about setting her room on fire. Aunt Karen says, "I don't want those damned kids around." I know that we are not safe. Is there any place that is safe?

After the fire, a social worker comes to Grandmo's. She is a white lady who tells me that it isn't safe here at Grandmo's. She says she has to take me to a new home, a foster home. My heart sinks into the pit of my tummy. Yasmin and Junior aren't there, and nobody will tell me where they are. I don't want to go anywhere until I can find them. The social worker walks me down the driveway of my Grandmo's house. I am crying, the anger and fear making me act like a baby instead of the nine-year-old I am. I get in her big, black four-door sedan. It's the kind of car I see in police shows. She says she is taking me to Mother Ackley's house. I don't know who that is, so she says, "It's only two blocks away." I don't care how close it is. That doesn't tell me who this person is. I ask, "Where are Yasmin and Junior?"

"They're in a safe place. Regina, you aren't going to live with them. They are in a different foster home, but it's not

54

too far from your new home," says the social worker. I hate social workers. I want to know why we can't be together. I'm beginning to welp up. I don't know what is going to happen to me and I don't know where my sister and brother are. I think they are supposed to be with me, so I can take care of them. Where are daddy and Frankie Mae? Where is *she*? I keep asking questions, and the social worker keeps telling me I am going to this foster home. I can't make her listen when I say I need to be with Junior and Yasmin. There is nobody who can make this lady take me where I'm supposed to be. I don't have a place where I'm supposed to be right now, but that's wherever Yasmin and Junior are. She then says, "You'll have brothers and sisters at your new house."

"They are not *my* brother and sister. Junior and Yasmin have never been away from me." I am yelling and crying, feeling like I need to do something but can't. I'm trapped in this big black car with this nice but mean lady. Her voice sounds like she is nice but what she is doing is really bad. I asked her why she was doing it. Did I do something wrong? Was it because my aunt set the fire, and nobody wanted all of us? All I can do is sit in the back of the car and cry. I become really mad knowing that Junior and Yasmin are not going to sleep in the same bed as me tonight. But at least they have each other, right? I asked the social worker that and she said yes, they will always be together because they are like twins. What does that mean? I don't ask.

"If I don't like it here, where will I go? Will I be able to go to where Junior and Yasmin are?" That idea makes me feel a little better. Maybe this isn't for real. Maybe it's just for a little while.

"This is going to be your new home. You'll like it here" as we quickly approached the house. The social worker still isn't listening to what I want. I should be used to everybody ignoring what I want, but this is really important. I need to make her see that. What I say doesn't matter. She just keeps driving.

It's only a short drive, not enough time for me to stop crying. But I hurry to wipe my tears because crying is embarrassing. In a few blocks and we are at the driveway of 107 Hill Street. When we get out of the car, the social worker takes a tissue out of her bag and wipes my tears. That's supposed to make me feel better, but it doesn't. "You're going to meet your new family," the social worker tells me. I don't want a new family. I want my *own* family. It's a big white house with green shutters like Grandmo's. The white lady social worker knocks on the door and the woman who she says I'm supposed to call Mother Ackley answers. She is short and dark, and she wears a wig. We walk inside and go into the living room where four kids are sitting looking at me.

I don't like any of this, but there is no place to hide from their stares. I have to just stand there and take whatever happens to me. If they talk to me, I will cry. My feelings are so hurt that I find a trick to turn off my mind. I tell myself, "This is not happening to me." I make myself go blank. That is the best way. Somehow, I know that I can't stop bad things from happening, no matter if I behave, if I am smart, if I go to church or dance. There's nothing I can do, so I become nothing. This is the way I have to be whenever anything bad happens. I have to stop the feelings and thoughts in my head. I think about Grandmo saying, "Baby, you're gonna be okay." That is the answer to all the bad things. I tell myself, "I'm gonna to be okay."

Mother Ackley introduces me as Regina to the two oldest, Ricky and Annette Payne, who are brother and sister. Annette is in middle school and Ricky is in high school. They just say hi. Then she introduces me to the five-year-old twins, who she had adopted, Trina and Trevor. I look at the two sets of kids, and I think they have their brother or sister. I have no one. And I'm right in the middle. That makes me want to cry again. But I don't in front of them. At least I got my name back.

The first thing Mother Ackley does is take me to the kitchen to offer me something to eat. She cooks me oatmeal. I eat so fast, and I just keep eating. At Grandmo's house, if you didn't get food fast, you didn't get any food. You had to get it before anybody else did.

"Baby, slow down. There's more food." But I can't slow down.

What is life going to be like here? At least it seems I won't have to fight for food. Yasmin and Junior aren't allowed to live in the same home with me, but they are allowed to visit.

The lady that my brother and sister live with is a grandma, too, but she doesn't do the regular things to take care of them. She doesn't even know how to comb my sisters' hair, so my sister and brother walk over to my foster home so I can do it. When I see Yasmin and Junior, I make sure to hug and kiss them. I tell them I love them and teach them to say, "I love you." I need to be sure they don't go through life with nobody loving them. I know how bad that feels.

Ricky, Annette, and me walk to church three times a week. Wednesday night is Bible study, and Friday night is prayer night. And sometimes on Saturdays if Annette is going to sing in the choir, we all walk together to take her to her choir rehearsal. By this time, I'm thinking church is what everybody is just supposed to do all the time. The walk to church is eight blocks and we pass my Grandmo's house each time. I want to stop in and see my Grandmo, but Ricky and Annette say no. We don't have time. Three blocks past Grandmo's are their mother's house. We sometimes stop there and stay the whole time we are supposed to be in church. We have time for that.

Ricky has a bike. He teaches me how to ride his bike on the long driveway. When he is outside, I run out to be with him. Even though he teases me, he is still nice, and he never tries to touch me, not like the pumping game or the kissing game. He is half black and half Mexican, the first person like that I have ever seen. He has lighter skin and big curly hair. Annette is dark because she has a different father, who is black, too. Nobody knows Annette's birthday because their mother was on drugs all the time and can't remember. That is worse than my daddy not believing in celebrating birthdays. They gave her the same day as Ricky's birthday.

Things aren't bad at Mother Ackley's house, but they aren't really good either. Mother Ackley is a good cook, and she cooks a lot. We all have chores to do, but not like at Grandmo's. Mother Ackley fusses mostly at Annette for sweeping the floor or getting the dishes clean. I have to make our beds and keep the upstairs floor clean in case Mother Ackley comes up to check on us. She never does.

There are two rooms upstairs, one for girls and one for boys. Mother Ackley and her husband sleep downstairs. There is a kitchen upstairs, too, like it is supposed to be a different apartment. The kitchen is where Annette presses my hair. I have long wavy hair, and Annette has almost no hair. She burns me at least once every time.

Pops is Mother Ackley's husband. He looks mean and scary. Tall, dark, just mean looking. When we are home, he stays at the back of the house in their bedroom just behind the kitchen. We are never allowed to go past the kitchen. He has a pickup truck. It seems like all the men with trucks pick up trash, so I think that must be what he does. I'm not sure, and Mother Ackley never talks about him. All I know is that most days he goes to work. He never eats with us. Mother Ackley cooks dinner and sets him a plate to eat by himself. The first day I came, Annette told me, "Just stay upstairs. Don't say nothing to him." I do what she tells me. I'm not sure why he is so scary. He doesn't spank or yell. Except one time he yells at Ricky because he had to go with Pops to work on weekends. It's safer just to stay away from him, even though it turns out he is not really mean. He just has nothing to do with me.

We are allowed to sit sometimes with Mother Ackley and watch tv—but never *Batman* or *Spiderman*, my two favorites. Mother Ackley makes us watch '*The 700 Club*'. There aren't a lot of shows to watch because of her religion. I spend my time reading books I get from school. Annette doesn't like to read, so she gets in trouble. Mother Ackley always asks her, "Why can't you be like Regina?" I feel proud. She even goes to my teacher conferences and the teachers tell her how great a student I am. Nobody at school ever says I am dumb or can't do something. But Annette and Ricky don't like it.

Ricky calls me "Big Bertha Butt." Annette laughs and joins in. Annette acts jealous of me. I was always the skinny one at Grandmo's, but my body is getting different now. Mother Ackley agrees with Ricky, calling me Big Butt, too. She tells me to bounce on my butt to make it smaller. She tells me to sit up straight with my hands on the floor on either side of my hips and bounce up and down every day. It hurts, and my butt doesn't get any smaller.

Ricky and Annette like to tease me about anything. They say, "Your mother doesn't want you. That's why you're here. And you can't even be with your sister and brother, but we can." As if it's my fault. Is it? It feels like an extra cruelty that I am living between two pairs of sisters and brothers, but I can't live with my own siblings. When I can't take it one day, I run away to Grandmo's house. Before I get through the door, Aunt Karen comes out on the porch. She doesn't want me there.

"You need to go back to your foster house. You don't live here. We aren't even supposed to be your family," she says. Grandmo must be at work. When I ask to stay, Aunt Karen cusses at me, and I have no choice but to go. I cried the whole way back, a couple of blocks through the alley, thinking it couldn't be true that they weren't my family. Mother Ackley isn't home when I get back, so she won't know to fuss at me about running away. I think Ricky and Annette will tell on me, but Mother Ackley doesn't say anything, so I guess I'm okay. Even though Mother Ackley has never spanked me, I'm scared of getting yelled at; it will make me cry. I have to behave.

At Christmas time there is a Christmas tree in the living room in front of the window, so you can see it in front from the wrap-around porch. Probably Trina and Trevor got to help decorate it while we were at school. I don't remember any Christmases when I was young. Daddy taught us that all holidays were something white men invented to make money. So, we never had any gifts or decorations like this and when we didn't celebrate at Grandmo's it just seemed normal not to.

The night before Christmas morning I am so happy. The presents are already under the tree, and we aren't allowed to touch anything. The idea of getting presents in the morning is new and exciting. I can barely sleep. When we get up, we sit in the living room to open our gifts. Trina and Trevor get several. I am a counter, loving to use numbers any way I can, but even if I wasn't, it isn't hard to count to the number one— how many presents I get. I open the gift wrap, tearing into this one precious package. The cover is colorful. It is a children's bible. Mother Ackley knows I love to read, and she knows I love God. It is a wonderful gift, but it is only one. *Did I tell her what my dad said about holidays? Or maybe I just don't deserve more? How many did Annette and Ricky get? Three each.* They are still opening up after I am done opening mine.

I had already learned about foster homes and about the pecking order of kids. First is Mother Ackley's grown-up daughter who lives down the street. Next are Trina and

59

Trevor— Mother Ackley's real kids because they were adopted by her when they were babies. They are more special than me. Ricky and Annette had been there five years. They are more hers than I am at this point. I go into my room to read my bible.

The bible is very important at Mother Ackley's house because she is very religious. Mother Ackley and us kids go to church all the time. Pops don't go to church ever. It's a different church than the one I went to with Grandmo, and they call it a Pentecostal church. I listen to the preacher very hard. No makeup, hems below your knees, no skating or dancing. He is against movies, but when *The Exorcist* comes out, he makes all the parents take their kids to see it. He says when you are bad, it's because you have demons. Trevor misbehaves a lot, so he has a demon. They would pray and put their hand on you to drive out the demons. I feel scared when I see that. Forgiveness is what I take from that church, over and over again. Because the preacher says Jesus says to forgive 7×7, I remember. I have to forgive no matter what. I have to forgive my cousins for teasing me and for the pumping game that scared me so much. I have to forgive Aunt Karen for burning us out of our family. I have to forgive *her* for leaving us.

That and never tell a lie. Because Jesus knows and bad things will happen. Lying is bad, and I vow never to do it. It's a hard promise to keep because I also have to keep all the secrets about what happened at home. I do my best. The preacher does a good job of telling us how Satan will get us if we lie. I don't want to be punished, so I am afraid. Even if I want to lie, I can't because the fear makes me stop. I can't let any more bad things happen to me or I don't know what I'll do. Every day, I'm afraid of what will happen because I think all the time about the worst things that I can endure. Then I think about some good things that might happen. *She* might come back. I might be able to live with Junior and Yasmin again. I try to have hope. If I do bad things, then nothing good can happen— that is what I have learned at church. It makes me feel afraid sometimes.

Otherwise, I love church because I love singing and I love dancing, and Pentecostal dancing is a holy dance. On Sundays, I go up to the front with all the others and dance, sometimes for too long. I close my eyes, and the singing and

60

organ music take me away. The drums and tambourines beat a rhythm that seems to carry me to someplace I have never been. My heart beats and I sway and clap until I imagine I'm in heaven. When I open my eyes, I can see that everybody else has stopped dancing. But I don't get in trouble and it's one of the few times I feel truly happy, so I don't think dancing for too long is bad. When you get the holy spirit, you dance the pastor says. I just danced because it made me happy. I don't know if that is the holy spirit or not. I don't really feel holy, but I do what the adults do. It's fun and no one tells me I have to stop. When grownups do the holy dance, the ushers come and fan them, so they don't get too hot. Somehow, they know when to stop, so the preacher can get back to his sermon and tell us what we aren't supposed to do.

I hear the adults say I have the Holy Spirit. What is the Holy Spirit? Is that the opposite of Satan? I remember the song I learned at Grandmo's church. We sing it here, too. "Jesus loves me, this I know." I want that to be true. I want to know if there is someone who loves me no matter what.

Mother Ackley follows all the rules the preacher says to. I'm not allowed to wear pants in this foster home. Dresses only. She gives me Annette's hand-me-down dresses, and sometimes she comes home with a bag that has a dress in it for me. We also can't go to movies, watch bad things on TV, or go skating or dancing. I can only listen to gospel music and not any of the music my daddy used to play.

In the summer, I ask for a bike and Mother Ackley says, "Let me think about it." Then one day, she says, "We're going to get you a bike." *I'm going to have a bike of my own!* She tells Ricky to come with us and we drive north on Hill Street. Then we turn onto Northwest Street. We keep passing houses, and I think we must be going to Parka Plaza. That is where all the stores are. I am nine years old, looking out the window, feeling like this is the longest car ride ever. I can't wait. We go past where we are supposed to turn to go to the store.

"I thought you were getting me a bike."

"We are. We're getting it right here."

Right after we go over the bridge, she slows down, turns on her blinker and pulls into a driveway.

I jump out of the car even before it is fully parked, and hear Mother Ackley calling, "Wait, Regina," but I am too excited to stop. She walks to the door and a lady comes out.

"We're here to get the bike you have for sale," Mother Ackley says, and I can't believe she is talking about my bike.

She pays the lady $10. The lady takes Ricky to the garage, and he walks the bike out to me. It's a tan boy's ten-speed. I grab the bike and say, "I have a bike!"

"Yes, but if you ever leave, you can't take it with you," Mother Ackley says. I don't care. I am so happy. I don't know when I felt this happy in a long time. Ricky ties it to the top of the car. As soon as we get home and Ricky takes it down, I jump on it. It's hard to get over the bar in my dress.

Ricky reminds me, "You can't take the bike when you leave." That doesn't matter to me because I don't expect to ever get to leave anyway. Adoption was talked about a while ago because a lady at church named Mrs. Once (my friend Brinnie's mom) wanted to adopt me, but that never happened.

After a while, Mother Ackley stops going to church with us anymore. On Sundays, she sends me and Ricky and Annette because we are old enough to walk there alone. We go on Sunday morning for Sunday school and stay for Sunday afternoon service. Then we walk home for dinner and go back to church for Sunday evening service. One day we get home from school and Pops tells us that Mother Ackley isn't there. That she has gone to heaven. Her daughter, Lida, is there holding the twins and they start to cry. I feel sad for Mother Ackley, but then I think maybe I can go to be with Yasmin and Junior now. I don't even notice Ricky and Annette.

Before Mother Ackley passed, I had already learned what death meant. My Grandmo's husband, George, died when I had been living at Mother Ackley's house for about a year. I was allowed to go to the funeral. I sat next to my cousins at the front of the church. I only saw them at school, so I was excited to be in the family section. I heard a clickety sound at the rear of the church. So, I looked up in that direction and saw my daddy walking shackled by foot and hands with a policeman on each side of him. I jumped up to go to him. Someone tried to hold me back, but I struggled to get away. I ran up to my dad to hug him. I hadn't seen him in so long I don't remember how long it's been since he went to jail.

Mother Ackley's funeral is different. I am not part of the family. Even though all five of us called her Mother Ackley, all five of us aren't the same. Trina and Trevor, being the adopted ones, get to ride in the big black car with her real daughter and Pops. I am not allowed to ride in the family car. I have to go to the funeral with someone else who I don't know. It hurts so bad to be told I am not family again. Ricky and Annette have to go in a different car, too, not the one I am in. I am sad she died. Nobody got us ready or even told us she was sick. I know she sat on the couch a lot and didn't go to church, but nobody said that meant she might die. I know she is not my mom. At school kids tease me because I am in foster care and my real mom didn't want me. At least I had Mother Ackley, but now I know for sure there is nobody who is my mama.

When the funeral is over, we go back to the house, and a lot of people are all around me, but no one really pays much attention to me so I kind of just go off to the corner and look out the window at Hill Street. I don't ask about moving and nobody tells me what is going to happen to me now. I sit, wondering what this means. Will I have to go to another foster home, and will I be able to take my bike? I'm too sad and confused to know what to do.

The next day a caseworker comes over and tells me that I will have to go to a new foster home. And I ask can I go live with my brother and sister. She says she doesn't know, but she'll see what she can do. She says I have to wait until she can get back to me, but I feel a little bit of hope. I went to bed that night scared and excited at the same time. Maybe I'll get to live with my brother and sister again. I won't have to wait until my sister gets to come over to get her hair done to see them. Maybe we can all go and live with our daddy again.

Chapter 10

Together Again

"My story can unchain someone else's prison." — Patricia Dsouza

I think maybe my daddy can finally get us again, but he is in prison a second time. He shot somebody else. My daddy is really married to a woman named Vanessa. She's the one who tried to get Junior and me at the Top-Notch party store. Daddy tried to shoot Vanessa.

My cousins tell me what happened when I see them at the school playground. I tell them I want to go live with my daddy now that I won't have a foster home anymore. They say, "You can't go live with your daddy. He's in jail again. He tried to shoot the lady he married to." My cousins like to talk about what they overhear their mamas say. They tell me about the white lady my daddy was married to all along and that my aunts call her "that white whore." They call my daddy her pimp. My cousins say one night daddy's best friend was at the house, and he decided his best friend wanted Vanessa, so daddy said he was going to shoot them both. His friend knew how to run. Vanessa stayed. Daddy came out of his room with a gun. Vanessa's daughter jumped in the way and got shot in the hip. The judge said he had to go to prison. I hate the judge.

"You lie!" I shout at my cousins. And I ran into the bathroom to cry.

I ask the social worker about my daddy, who she says isn't my daddy, and she tells me he is married to that white lady, not Frankie Mae, and he's in jail. She is going to take me to Yasmin and Junior. That makes me a little happier. I get to pack all my stuff in brown paper bags, but when I go to get my bike, Ricky steps in front of me and says, "Remember, Mother Ackley said you couldn't take your bike?" If Ricky hadn't stepped in, I could have taken it. His bike had had a flat for a while—and now he gets to keep mine. Sometimes he used to take my bike to go to his friends' houses and Mother Ackley wouldn't say anything. I would sit on the porch and cry until he came back. I think he thinks it's his bike now. Leaving my bike makes me sad, but I am so happy about going to live with

Yasmin and Junior to cry now. Nothing is more important than that. Nothing, not even my bike.

In the car driving to Yasmin and Junior's foster home, the social worker says, "Like I said, we're able to let you go to the Carpenter house, but you must promise me this."

I ask, "What?"

She says, "You won't boss your sister and brother around. Do you understand what bossing means?" I'm ten, and I know what bossy is, but she tells me anyway. "Well, they have a foster mother just like you had, and she's the one to tell them what they're to do, and that means you can't tell them what to do also. Their foster mother is like their mom. She gets them ready for school, she feeds them, and they call her grandma. You'll need to call this lady Grandma too."

"I have a grandma already,' I say.

"I know but that grandma is not really your grandma."

"What do you mean my grandma's not really my grandma?"

"Well because your dad isn't really your dad." She says my mom and dad weren't married when I was born. His name isn't on my birth certificate, so he isn't legally my dad. That makes no sense. I call him Daddy. He is the one who we lived with when all of us were born. He is the one who took me to preschool. We have the same last name. The social worker doesn't listen. She just says that if my daddy isn't my daddy, then Grandmo isn't my grandmother. Without legal papers, I belong to nobody.

"My dad IS my daddy." I don't know what this lady is talking about. She just sits there silently, and I feel confused and hurt. How can she tell these lies to me? I know what a lie is. God is not going to like her for saying these things to me. It's like she's saying I don't even exist. Like whom I am isn't who I am. It makes me want to scream and punch someone. But I have to be happy right now. I am going to live with my sister and brother. It's been way too long. Way too long. I was eight when we lived together at Frankie Mae's and now, I'm almost eleven.

When I get to the new home, the lady I'm supposed to call Grandma shows me where I'll sleep. Junior and Yasmin sleep in a bed together. I am to sleep on a cot to next to them.

There are just three bedrooms, and all the other rooms are taken. The room for their son Bradley has two beds in it, and the grownup room has a lock on the door. The grandma lady tells me I'm never supposed to go in there. Her real name is Enola Carpenter. She always has a Pepsi can in her hand. She's a tall lady with light skin and she has a big chest, but it looks like she isn't wearing a bra. She looks nice, but I have this feeling about her that she isn't, maybe she's acting that way because the white lady social worker is still there. Bradley is adopted, but he has been her son since he was born. He's 15 now, almost five years older than me. He goes to high school, and I am in 6th grade. I still have to go to Helmer Elementary. Grandma Carpenter has another grown daughter who lives down the street. She has two little girls, one is Yasmin 's age, and they play together, and one is younger.

Only Grandma sleeps in the locked room, and Grandpa, which is what we have to call her husband, shares a room with twin beds with their son Bradley. That seems weird, but everybody acts like it's normal. Grandpa's work is driving the truck to pick up trash. He is tall and big. I think he looks scary, but he doesn't say anything to me or any of the other kids. I know from Yasmin and Junior that he never talks to the kids. At first, the only time we see Grandpa is when he comes home after driving the truck, eats the meal Grandma made him, sits alone at the table, and then goes into the living room to watch tv. It's a lot like what Pops did at Mother Ackley's.

Grandma Carpenter had been a foster mother for years. Her work is taking care of foster kids. Yasmin and Junior tell me that Grandma is very strict, especially about where you can go and not go in the house. They think it's funny she sleeps in the grown-up bedroom and nobody else goes in there. Grandma has a lot of rules, but I have enough food, so that is good. Also, Yasmin and Junior say they are not whipped like Grandmo's.

Every week we do the same things. School, home, dinner, bed. We are allowed to sit on the couch if we ask first, otherwise, we have to sit on the floor. All the furniture is covered with plastic to protect it from us. The living room is for company, but I only ever see Grandma talking to people through the front door, mostly people from her church. We go to church, but not all the time like Mother Ackley's. We try to stay outside when we can. On Saturday afternoons, if she is in the mood, Grandma Carpenter takes us in her station wagon to the Salvation Army to pick out clothes. I hate going because I don't like wearing a stranger's clothes and used shoes. My friends can tell. They tease me about Salvation Army clothes at school. At least I get to wear pants. This grandma says it's not a sin. What about new clothes? One day I am going to have new clothes like the ones my daddy would buy. The last time I had clothes of my own was when we lived with Daddy and Frankie Mae. They don't fit me anymore.

I am in fifth grade and go into sixth grade while I live at the Carpenter house. Two of my classmates from fifth grade are still in my class this year. Their names are Bella and Nini. Bella's parents let me spend the night sometimes when Grandma Carpenter will let me go. Grandma Carpenter doesn't even care if it's a school night, not sure why. Yasmin plays with Grandma Carpenter's granddaughters and Junior plays with the boy across the street. They have friends, so I don't feel like I am abandoning them.

Nobody is allowed to stay at my foster home, but they can walk over to get me to go back to their houses. Bella's parents are really nice, even though they don't talk to each other. They are strict about rules, but that is because they care about Bella. I feel jealous of Bella's family with a mom and a dad, plus they have three kids and take care of their niece. This is how a family looks, kind of like when we lived with Frankie Mae. I want a family like this again, but at least I have Yasmin and Junior now. Nini's mom talks to me. Bella's mom doesn't talk much but her cousin does. She asks me a lot of questions.

Nini lives next to Bella, and sometimes she asks me to spend the night, too. Nini has an older sister. Her house just has two bedrooms. Bella's house looks like Nini's but it's better to stay there because they have an upstairs where we can watch tv. My daddy told me a long time ago that *she* was a singer, so whenever we watch tv I try to see *her*. I tell Bella and Nini what my daddy said about how *she* left us to become a famous singer. Every time I see a black woman singing on TV, I think it's *her*. Bella and Nini help me look, but it's hard because I don't have a picture, and I barely remember what *she* looks like anymore. I try to imagine the face that is sitting in the back of that taxi driving away from me and Junior, leaving us all at

Grandmo's like we don't matter. I'm sure I'll recognize *her.* One time we saw the Pointer Sisters on a show, and I am sure one of them is *her.* Bella and Nini laughed at me. "They are all sisters," they say. "If she is your mama, then all the other ones are your aunts." I want to cry, but I can't because then they will know how sad it makes me. Then I will know the lady on tv is not my mother.

In school, we have an assignment to write a book. I'm very excited. We sit in class and make covers by putting fabric over cardboard. My fabric is yellow, which is a happy color. We are supposed to staple the pages on the inside. A lot of the kids are messing around, but I am happy about making my first real book. I love books so much, and I love to write. I am going to keep the book I make with me forever, just like the bible. Any time I am sad, I have the bible Mother Ackley gave me to read. I read anytime I can. I get books from our school library. Though, I don't know any books by black people, but my book will be one.

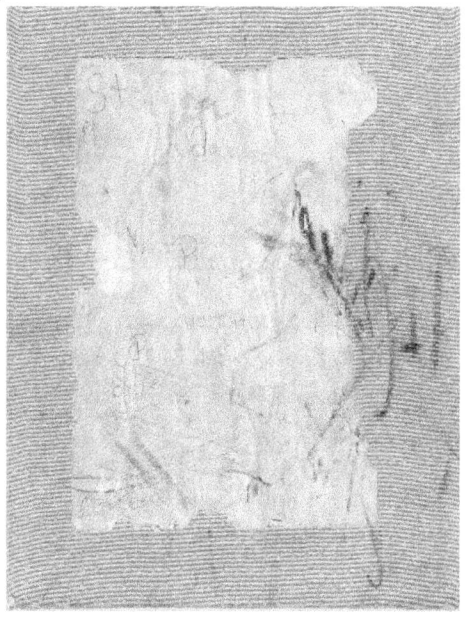

I want to make it look like a real book, so I put in all the things that are in my books, like the title and drawings. It is called *Stories and Poems by Regina Moore*. Illustrated by R. Moore. Printed by Moore and Company, Incorporated, Boston, Massachusetts. That looks official. I draw all of the pictures and write in my neatest handwriting, so it looks pretty.   The book has stories and riddles and poems. When I hand it in, my teacher writes a nice message in it. She signed it: "We had a great year, Regina. Hope all of your years are great, Mrs. James." That makes the book even better.

There is no lock on our door. I am lying in bed drifting off to sleep when I feel a presence hovering over me. It's just Grandpa, coming to check on me to see if I am sleeping. But he never does that, and he doesn't seem to care about things like if I eat or sleep or even exist.

He puts his hand over my mouth and whispers, "Shhhhh." Then he takes his hand and starts to pull down my underpants. I try to squirm away, but my bed is against Yasmin and Junior's bed, and he is on the other side, so he has me blocked in. Even though I don't know the secrets everyone else seems to know, I know he shouldn't be touching my underpants. I put my hands down to try to block him, but he brushes my hands away and gives me the look of a parent who is punishing a kid. I know it's a look I'll never forget. What is he trying to do? This can't be right. But I have been taught to obey adults.

He whispers, "Don't say anything." And then he leans down over the bed and puts his mouth on my privates. I feel shame and shock. I don't know what to do, how to make it stop, what he expects from me. This is worse than Tyrone and Maddox. They didn't take my panties off. Panic and fear overwhelm me. I make my mind go blank and I tell myself I'm going to be okay. It seems to last forever. But then he just walks out the door. I hope Yasmin and Junior are asleep through this.

Am I to go to sleep now? What happened? What was that? These questions whirl around in my head until I finally fall asleep. I get up the next morning and hurry to school without talking to anyone in the house. When I get to school, I feel different, and I'm sure a teacher or the principal will know what happened. I hope somehow, they do know because I was told not to tell anyone so there's no way to ask for help. I remember the half-naked beating I got from Grandmo after telling my teacher I didn't have food for lunch. So, I know I can't say anything.

I wonder if I should tell Bella or Nini, or will they just know? But nothing happens. It's like life is just supposed to keep on going the way it always has even though this horrible thing happened. The only thing I know for sure is that I am afraid to go to bed again. If I could, I would take Yasmin and Junior away from there, but we don't have any place else to go.

The case worker said that my dad wasn't my dad, so my aunts aren't my aunts and Grandmo isn't my grandmother. The only home I have to go back to is the one where Grandpa lives. I'm afraid to go back into that cot. I am scared Grandpa will come again. And he does.

When it's the weekend, Grandpa tells Grandma, "I'll take the girl with me today. She can help, earn her keep."

"Please, I want to stay here. I have homework to do," I say, looking at Grandma, hoping she will take my side. But she doesn't, so I go to my room to get dressed for a day of picking up garbage. I would have loved it if I had been there to pick up garbage. I am used to working, to making myself useful so I won't be a burden, so people will want me around. But that was never Grandpa's intention. For the whole day, I sit next to him in the front seat of the truck and he touches me in that place again with his ugly fingers, seeming to enjoy making me sit there while cars pass us, making me wait while he jumps out to dump the garbage cans into the back (because even though he had said I was going to help, I can't get out of the car at every stop with my pants down). I try to make my mind go blank and tell myself that I am going to be okay. When will I ever be okay?

Week after week, Grandpa comes to my room at night and then comes down to breakfast on Saturday mornings and says he needs me to help him on his run. Week after week, I plead to get out of it, saying I am supposed to go to Bella's house or anything I can think of. There's no way to tell if he is going to make me go do trash or if I will be safe for a day. I'm afraid to go to bed at night, and I'm afraid to get up every morning because not knowing somehow seems worse. There's little hope but then that hope is killed, like the man my daddy hung from a pole. It's better to make myself go blank, to make myself feel nothing. If I had my daddy, he would shoot Grandpa and hang him from a pole, but I don't have anybody. I know I can't tell Grandma the real reason—I feel too much shame, and I can't figure out what I am doing to make this terrible thing happen. Grandpa already said nobody would believe me. I know that I will be the one in trouble if the truth is told.

One afternoon, I saw again what violence really looks like. I also learn how mad I can get. This is worse than daddy pointing a gun. It's even worse than getting whooped. It's like when Theo hit Yasmin with a rock. I have so many bad things to keep track of that I can barely say what is worse than what anymore. This time, it's Junior, and the boy isn't family. Dolan, the boy who lives next door to our foster home, and Junior get in a fight. They fight about all kinds of things, just like boys, but this time is worse. I can hear the yelling but I'm playing on the porch and figure it's just the boys. They are on the driveway between the houses, and I run over there when I hear Junior scream. It looks like Dolan had run in his house and come out with scissors. I couldn't believe it; he stabbed Junior in the chest.

There is blood all over Dolan's hand with the scissors and on Junior's chest. Junior can't breathe; he's panting in a funny way. I ran into the house to tell Grandma. She runs out to see what happened and then goes back in to call an ambulance. I follow and stay outside with Junior. I say, "Junior, you are going to be ok. Don't close your eyes." This is the same thing I remember from when Yasmin got hit with the brick. When the ambulance comes, the guys make me move. I don't want to leave Junior, but Grandma pulls me away. One of the white guy's cuts Junior's shirt open to see the stabbing. They put a mask over his face, and one of them says the stab wound missed his lungs by only an inch. They seem to think that is a good thing, but all I see is my brother bleeding on the driveway. They put him in the big lighted truck with the loud siren to rush him to the hospital. Just like they did to Yasmin.

I think to myself this is not happening again. I know I didn't protect my brother like I didn't protect my sister. Daddy always told me to watch over my little brother and sister, but bad things keep happening, and I can't stop them. I feel so angry and sad. I'm angry at myself, not just Dolan. My daddy would be disappointed in me. I want to cry and scream. I want to go back and do something different, something that would make all this go away, except I don't know what that is. And that makes me angrier, and I feel sad that Junior will be there alone.

After the ambulance leaves, Dolan hides inside his house. So, I wait. I wait until school the next day. I am going to hurt him really bad. He should see what it's like to not be able to breathe, like he did to Junior. When we get to school before the bell rings, Dolan is playing in the playground just like all the other kids. I started to run at him, and he ran away. I'm not gonna let him get away with this, so I chase him down. When I catch him, I knock him over and start beating on him. I pound and pound him while a circle of kids gathers around to cheer me on. I hit as hard as I could, over and over, and each hit feels good—and I haven't felt good in a long time—like hitting one of the people who had hurt us and left us. I can't protect them, but this is the first time I can punish the person who hurt them. All of a sudden, Dolan is all the things that are making life bad. I beat him the way I wanted to hit the social worker, and Frankie Mae, and *her*. I keep beating him, like the judge who put daddy away and Aunt Karen who was so mean, and Uncle Tommy and my cousins, and Grandpa. This is a lot of people, and I do a lot of punches. I don't stop until teachers pull us apart. We are taken to Mr. Green's office.

He says, Regina, you've been to this school off and on for years, and you've never been in trouble. Why would you do this?"

"He stabbed my brother, and he almost died," I yell, trying to hold back the tears of anger and frustration.

"You don't bring your home to school."

"What else could I do? He wouldn't come outside." Mr. Green doesn't have an answer either. Instead, he tells me what my punishment is. But I don't care. I just want my brother to be okay and Dolan to pay for what he did. The punishment is that I have to eat lunch every day in Mr. Green's office with Dolan until we make up. Talk and act friendly, I guess. Dolan doesn't come to school the next day. But the day after that he came with a cast on his arm. I guess I broke his arm. Mr. Green starts our punishment. We hold out for a couple of weeks until I pretend to get along with him so I can go to recess. It's one of the only good things I get to do, playing on the monkey bars and twirling. Dolan says sorry, too, but I know he doesn't mean it.

Junior is out of the hospital but not at school yet. I know Dolan is scared of me now, so he doesn't come outside to play anymore. Then we find out that he was sent away, either to another foster home or juvie, nobody knows.

Chapter 11

Visiting Daddy

"A daughter should not have to beg her father for a relationship."—Jack Kerouac, poet.

One Saturday, the lady who tried to get us from the party store came to get me. She says she is daddy's wife, which is crazy because what about Frankie Mae? But that just means that what my cousins told me was true. I don't care because she says she can take me to see my daddy. I don't know if Grandma Carpenter will let me, but I beg, and the lady whose name is Vanessa gives Grandma Carpenter something, and Grandma lets me go. The last time I saw Daddy was at my grandpa's funeral--that was the last time I saw anyone in my family except my cousins on the school playground. If Vanessa is my dad's wife, she is my family, even if she is white.

Every Saturday that Vanessa comes to get me after I "work" with Grandpa, I run from the truck to get into her car as fast as I can. I am so happy to get away that I don't even mind leaving Yasmin and Junior for a few hours. I know Yasmin and Junior are too little and will be with Grandma Carpenter, not Grandpa.

I know my daddy is in prison, and I've seen prisons on tv, but I never really thought it was real until now. Everything here is strange. We drive up through a gate and then we go to this fenced-in area. There is a large building then a small bone with picnic tables in from in a long line. My daddy is sitting at one of the tables and I take off running to him. He hugs me really tight, but a guard comes over and tells me to sit on the other side of the table. My daddy is wearing a prison uniform like all the other men, but I just see his face and his smile. He is crying, just like me. I am so happy that I don't have time to be mad. Most of the time, I am mad about the people who put daddy in jail, the police, and the judge. I am mad at the people who say he is not my father, and I have to be in foster care. They made all the bad things happen.

"Why can't Yasmin and Junior come?" I say. It's my job to take care of them, so I always have to think of them.

"You know I want to see them, too, Regina, but they're too young," he says. I am happy that I am old enough now that I'm twelve. He asks me about them, and I say they are fine because I don't want to tell him about Junior. He asks if I'm watching out for them, and I say I am doing my best. My best isn't good enough. But I don't want to say that. I let him and Vanessa talk for a while, and I looked around at the prison. It's scary and I don't want to think about my daddy being locked up in there. Such a big building with small windows.

"Can I come again?" I will ask when we are leaving after the first visit. I feel so sad, I can't stop crying. I'm not allowed to hug my daddy because the guards are watching. Vanessa says she will come and get me on Saturdays so I can visit. That makes me feel a little better.

We go to Vanessa's after leaving the prison. I'm worried about Yasmin and Junior, but she lives close to the prison and says we should stop by before I go back. I get to play with Autumn, her daughter who is fourteen, just a couple years older than me. Really playing with Autumn means going out to the railroad tracks so she can smoke with her friends. I would rather be with Yasmin and Junior.

Vanessa's house has an upstairs like Grandmo's with a pointy roof and enclosed porch. Vanessa is rich because before she married my daddy, she worked at a factory, I heard my aunts say. She had three fingers that got cut off and they had to give her a lot of money. The front yard is small, but the backyard is big, and they have a swing set back there, just like rich people. Upstairs there are lots of bedrooms, enough for all her kids to have their own beds. This makes me feel jealous. I still share a room with Yasmin and Junior and sleep on a cot. Vanessa has five kids. The three oldest girls are white. One of them is married and doesn't live there. Vanessa fights a lot with the oldest one who is still at home. Her son is a year younger than me. His dad built the house, says Vanessa, and they all have the same last name, but the baby girl is part black. There's a dining room that's fancy and a family room where everyone watches tv. It is a nicer house than either of my foster homes. I am lucky to get to play there, but feel bad that Yasmin and Junior can't come, just like they can't come to the prison. I tell them it's not so great because I don't want them to feel bad because they miss Daddy, too. I still don't know why Vanessa came to get me.

Vanessa has a copy of a newspaper that she has saved. I look at the article that says my daddy shot her daughter Autumn; the same story my cousins told me. Autumn was in a wheelchair before I met her, but now she can walk. She has a limp because the bullet hit her on the hip. Autumn never talks about my dad. Vanessa either. I don't know why Vanessa stays with my dad. I only care that they have my daddy, and I have to live with other people. They are spoiled--they have rooms and beds and a mom and once he gets out of prison, they will have **my** dad.

Life at the Carpenters is getting back to normal. Junior comes back from the hospital and gets better. I have my friends and my sister and brother. I make sure to kiss them and hug them. I am the oldest, and I think it will be better for them if they know someone older loves them. I feel happy when Grandpa isn't around.

Close to Christmas, the social work lady comes and has me stand outside so she can take a picture. They want someone to adopt me, to adopt all of us. She takes pictures of Yasmin and Junior, too. Then she takes a picture of all of us together. She gives us each a copy of our own picture. I wonder if they are 'for sale' pictures? I know foster parents get money for us. Will adopted parent to? On the back of my picture, she wrote "Regina M, age 11." Why didn't she spell out by last name? Is it because I'm not supposed to be my daddy's daughter. She also writes Jackson, Mich. Why? I don't think a lot about adoption because I don't believe there is anything better anymore. I try to be happy when I can and to make my mind go blank when Grandpa is there. That's the only thing I can do, that and try to keep Yasmin and Junior safe.

I still love school, learning and playing outside, except that something happens in the spring that makes me sad. We were playing on the playground when Bella and Nini told me I have to kiss this boy. They are going to kiss boys, too. I feel like I have to be like them, so on the playground, I go over and kiss my boy. Bella and Nini don't kiss their boys. They laugh at me and call me fast. I am so hurt by their reaction. The church I went to at Mother Ackley's taught me what 'fast' meant. Is there something in my behavior that makes people think I am fast? Peter *kissed* me. I don't even like boys yet— they just talk about me. I am told because I am skinny and have a big bootie, they pay attention to me only to tease me. They call me Big Bertha Butt, just like Ricky did. I hate to be bullied. But I have to take it, or I won't have friends. It is getting near the end of the school year, and of all the things I learn that year, the most important thing is that I am a follower. I will do what people tell me. I decided that I am not going to be like that anymore when I go to middle school.

It's time for us to meet a new family who want Yasmin and Junior and me. Those pictures we took out in the cold without our coats must have worked. It's summer now. The social worker comes to pick us up. She says we are going to a park in Lansing because it is halfway. It takes almost an hour to get there, and I wonder where you end up after another hour's drive for the other half of the way. I am too scared to ask anyone. What if these people don't like us? It doesn't seem like this can be for real. Part of me doesn't care what happens to us, but some part of me thinks that whatever this family is like, at least they would get me out of the Carpenter house. No more Grandpa. No more night visits.

We pulled up to this park. They are under a shelter at a picnic table. The tall dark guy with the bald head must be the daddy. He looks mean, though he tries to make a smile. The short light-complected lady is introduced as the new mama. She is not my mama, and she is not Yasmin and Junior's mama. I have already decided that I will never call anyone mama again. There is this little girl of about five. She needs her hair combed. Her hair looks like what Yasmin 's looked before I'd comb it. And there he is, a teenage boy, a man really. He has a lot of hair on his face and is very dark. I guess this completes the Carpenter family. That is what the social worker says their name is. Are they related to the Carpenter we are already living with? I hope not. Could the dad be like Grandpa? He looks like Grandpa, and he has the same last name. I have never heard of another black family being called Carpenter. I pray to Jesus they are not kin.

We get out of the car, and the little girl runs immediately to Yasmin. They hug and start playing. The girl's name is Shay. The social worker introduces me to the man and the woman, saying this will be your mom and this will be your dad, and finally Doug. I just nod because I'm not going to tell them that I won't be calling anyone Mama or Daddy. They can't make me, can they? Adults always get their way, it seems. It doesn't really matter what I think.

Even at twelve, I understand we are nobody's, just the property of the State of Michigan. I hated that. I hated that there was no *her*, no Daddy, no Grandmo. Did they all just turn their backs on us once the social worker said we weren't family? Did they not want to be bothered? I help take care of Yasmin and Junior, so it would not be that bad to take care of us, right? It hurts but I have to be strong for my sister and brother. They at least had me. I will never leave them. No, never. I decided right then I will forever take care of them. They are not going to know life without me. Skip *Her*, Daddy, and Grandmo. My sister and brother are the only ones to matter to me from now on. I'm not going to like this new family. Nope, not one bit.

I am just going to sit at the picnic table and not talk. While Yasmin and Shay play, Junior talks to Doug. He seems happy because at our other house, Bradley is never nice to him. Bradley is 16, and he's too busy to pay attention to a kid. If he does, he just picks on Junior. Doug seems really nice, even though he is only about a year older than Bradley. Junior, who is just 10, would be really happy to have a big brother. I still can't make myself happy. The social worker talks to the man. He tries to ask us questions about what we like to do and how we like school. I have no choice but to answer him. I admit that I like school.

The mama-lady doesn't say anything. I am sure not going to call her mama. I don't even call the lady who left us, mama, it's *her,* when I think about her. Not anymore. And what if these Carpenters are somehow related to the Carpenters we already live with? I can't get rid of that idea, and it makes me madder. There can't be anything good about this, other than getting away from Grandpa. That should be enough, but if I am sent to these people, I will never visit my dad again, never see my cousins at school, never see Bella and Nini. I try to think about what is better or worse. Nothing is better or worse. It's all bad. It seems like if I don't want something to happen, it's gonna happen for sure. It's not okay. Will I ever be, okay? I sit through the picnic for an hour, tuning them out, trying to last until it is time to drive back. I wanted Bella's family to adopt me, and I wanted the church lady, but they didn't want Yasmin and Junior. And I couldn't live with that.

The social worker told us the whole drive over that this was the best thing that could happen to us. I know, somehow, this is real. And there's nothing I can do about it. There's nothing I can do about anything. When the picnic is over, the social worker drives us back to the Carpenter foster home. I shudder as I walk through the door. I don't know how long I will have to stay here, and I don't know how I will live through more nights and more Saturdays. But this is the only place we have right now. I think again about how I don't have any choices. I like the books I read where the kids solve mysteries and figure things out. I wish I could figure this out.

The last horrible thing I remember about that foster home is the night I fell asleep on the couch watching tv. I wake up with him on top of me, his weight crushing me into the couch cushions. My pants are pulled down and he is trying to stick his privates between my legs, but not like Maddox and Tyler did. I feel pain down there that I have never felt before. I don't even know what he's doing with his privates, but it's terrible.

"Grandpa, you're hurting me," I yell, awake to the idea that there are more things he can do to me than what he has done before. This time, my sister saved me. She had been spending the night at his daughter's house up the street with one of her daughters when she decided to run away. She comes to the door and knocks really loudly, stopping Grandpa, in the act before he can finish with me. When he jumps back from the surprise of her knock on the door, I lunge away and run upstairs, Yasmin following right behind me, asking, "What's wrong, Regina?" Instead of answering her I asked her why you come back in the middle of the night. She says that she and the girls got into a fight, so she left. My sister, so brave. I said you shouldn't be walking alone in the dark. But that night I was really glad she did.

The next morning, I started packing the little clothes I had and my book. I packed some of Junior and Yasmin's clothes, too. I am not sure when we will leave but I want to be ready.

Chapter 12

I Feel Angry All the Time

**"If you're always trying to be normal, you will never know
how amazing you can be."
—Maya Angelou**

The social worker comes to our house and tells us that
after meeting us, the other Carpenter family chose us. The
social worker explains that they will be our new foster family.
All I feel is anger, instant anger. They are the only family she
introduced us to, so we don't have any other choice. I still can't
shake that they have the same name, Carpenter. None of that
matters because the grownups have already decided. The
social worker says that we are to be fostered for a year, and
then adopted.

I sat and talked with Yasmin and Junior. What do you
y'all think about moving to a new home? Being with the last
family, last move? Junior liked having a big brother. Yasmin,
just 9 years old now, said I'm sure I like this. I responded we
must give it a try because the social worker is so happy about it
and says we're lucky because they want all three of us.

Before I know it, we are moving to Grand Rapids,
Michigan. I must tell Bella and Nini that I am moving away.
They are so sad that Bella asks her parents to adopt us again,
but they don't have room for three kids. At our foster home,
nobody seems to say anything. Grandma Carpenter gives us
brown grocery bags to pack our things, one each. I help
Yasmin and Junior pack the clothes they have. I don't have
much. I packed the rest of my Salvation Army clothes even
though I hated them. Putting them in the paper bag is like
throwing them in the garbage. I wish I could be doing that
instead. I also pack my bible from Mother Ackley next to the
book I wrote for school and packed earlier.

We drove highway 127 for a short while that got us to
Lansing like last time. But this time we went west onto 96. I
know my highways because when on long trips with Dad I paid
a lot of attention to billboards and read every green sign. I

learned the little number signs were mile markers. So, you know how many miles from one town to another you could keep up without waiting on the big green sign to tell you many miles to the next town. And I knew how far we had to go. The judge said we have to be 100 miles away from Jackson, Michigan. Wouldn't you know Grand Rapids was exactly 100 miles away (northwest) from Jackson. I mean we could have landed 100 miles north of Jackson, but that would have been all white towns past Flint or Saginaw. Anyway, 100 miles wasn't going to keep me from my daddy EVER as I saw it. I know about trains and can learn about buses. I can run away back to him. But I wouldn't leave Junior and Yasmin. So, I'll have to plan it carefully one day. Back to present reality…to today…to how soon my life will change. I did not get good great vibes from these people or just because I DID NOT want to call another woman 'Mama' a stranger and a person for the next 6 years of my life. Jesus, I know you love me but is this family going to be good? I guess I'll have to wait and see. No one can make me think of Doug as my brother and Shay as my sister. Because they are not. Yasmin and Junior are my only kin. Always have been and always will be. We have to be closer than ever now. It's us against them. Like when I was in the Ackley house. I wasn't related to anyone…I did not call them my sister or brother, though I had to call Mrs. Ackley, Mother Ackley. I learned at from church not to cuss but damn it, here we go again. I don't want it, and I am going to find a way back to my daddy. I have little hope our real mother, "She" would come get us. After all it was explained to me the State of Michigan are our guardians (and has been for four years), until this new family adopts us in a year. And they still won't be out of the picture but will check in once in a while. I don't believe that. They are going to run like everyone else in my life.

When we get to our new house, it doesn't feel like a real home, it *looks like* it. The living room furniture is red, a couch and loveseat. They have a big dining table for six, like Grandmo's. The kitchen was big, at least to me. Stove in corner but fridge by back door…odd place I thought. And to the right of the dining room was a den. Hadn't really known of this room. So, I asked and was told it's where the family watches TV together. Um. I thought, ok. I didn't watch much TV at

Mother Ackley or the other Carpenter house. It might be ok. Not enough yet to change my angry feelings into happy ones. But I suppose I can pretend I am happy or glad. I'm not a good actor. People said I'm sensitive. I guess that means I cry a lot or easily. I do. I don't want to be in another new home or in the new school. I want to yell at Daddy Mark and Mama Betty, "You are not my family." I'm not related to you, and I don't even know these people. Of course, I could never yell at adults, no matter what they did. I don't want to call someone else Mama, and I don't see Daddy Mark as a father, though he says we are supposed to call him Daddy. This new guy is nothing to me but a stumbling block to getting back where I want to be, with my own daddy.

The 'tour' continues to the upstairs. I definitely want to see the sleeping arrangements: there are three bedrooms. Me, Yasmin and Shay are going to share a large pink room. I even got my own bed. 'a good sign'. Doug and Junior will share the smaller blue painted room. The parents sleep together in a room just down the hall. I think that might be a good thing. The dad won't be able to leave in the night without the mom knowing. There is a bathroom upstairs, too.

The first week there, we were taken to a big family park called Johnson Park. I'd never seen a park so big. We played kickball with each other and some kids at the park. Girls against the boys. We ate barbeque hot dogs and potato salad at the picnic table. It was really fun. I wonder is this like what a family is supposed to do.

Within a couple of months, I think it may not be such a good home. We're in the den. Mama and Shay with Junior, Yasmin and me. We're all watching Wheel-of-Fortune. I loved that game. Guessing puzzles. And I was good at it, too. Shay walks over to me and out of the blue, slaps the crap out of me. She is only five so I don't I can't hit her back. It stung me and my feelings were so hurt. I hadn't said anything to her or anyone but guessing the puzzle out loud. Mama Betty watches and starts laughing instead of telling her how naughty that was. My feelings were so hurt. I wanted to cry but I couldn't let Mama or Shay see me cry. So, I said I am going to bed and go upstairs to 'our' room. I am glad she didn't follow, but then again wouldn't Mama tell her to come and say I am sorry? No, she didn't, nor come up and see how I was doing. I began to get angry, angrier because I knew this was not going to be a good home. I knew it. Why did I think being here was going to be so good.

By the time the new social worker comes, she is still a white lady, things gotten worse. Now Yasmin and Junior get whippings, often. Junior for calling Shay names and Yasmin for wanting a toy Shay had or not agreeing with her. I know no one thinks it's enough to say it's abuse. Then again no one seems to care about what we think. So, on one of her monthly visits, I beg her to take us away. I tell her that these people don't treat us fairly and about the whippings but not the slap (I was too embarrassed). Sometimes Yasmin and Junior got whipped twice for one name calling because the mom would whoop them and then when the dad came home, she would give him a report and he would whip them again. It was way worse than how they were beaten at Grandmo's.

Yes, I must call them Mama and Daddy. But I just pretend it's ok and do my best to not say their names. As far as I'm concerned, they never will be our parents. "A family who wants to adopt all three of you is great, Regina," the social worker says. I decided in my head she wouldn't hear nothing I said. We're stuck.

One night there was a really bad thunderstorm. It feels weird to be in this new room with everything that is strange. Even though Yasmin is sleeping nearby, I feel like a deep fear is overtaking me. The room is dark and the noise from the storm rattles the windows and makes all the normal bedroom furniture scary. I have never been afraid of a thunderstorm before, but now, I know I can't stay in this room awake feeling so alone. I swallow my anger and hatred and go to Daddy Mark and Mama Betty's room. I knock on the door and ask if I can sleep in there during the storm. They let me sleep at the foot of the bed. It is amazing to me that I feel comforted and safe. The next day, I go back to my own room and get dressed and go back to my regular life and my regular feelings. But there is a little voice that is telling me that this house might be better. Maybe Grandmo was right, and I am going to be okay. There might be hope. I am going do my best to being open to it.

Doug, my new big *brother*, is five years older than me. A senior in high school. I don't like him because he calls me "Big Bertha Butt," just like Ricky did. When I cry, he calls me Jan Brady because he says I am just like the girl on *The Brady Bunch*--I cry when somebody talks about me. I hate Doug. I don't want another brother; I just want my own family. Plus, he turns Junior against me because Junior joins in picking on me about my butt. I can't take it out on Doug, so when they tease me, I hit Junior and run upstairs. No one gets a whipping for that. Or even yelled at.

Eventually, I see how nice it is that Doug treats Junior like a brother. This makes me happy to see because Junior was happy. Even when they have chores, Daddy Mark makes them do it together. That is better than it used to be, but I know I still have to be the one to protect Junior and Yasmin. Sometimes Doug talks to me and is nice. He even starts to tell me secrets about his parents little by little. It's so nice to have someone talk to me like a friend. Though he never asks me about other foster homes or my dad, I begin to tell him anyway. He appears to be listening. So, I start to feel inside, there is a little drop of hope. Hope that feels like music on record player and the volume low. But as you turn it louder, the music becomes so strong that it makes you want to dance. Doug loves music and make me remember I do too.

Sometimes Doug teaches us all to play cards, Spades and Tunk were my favorite. I learned about Monopoly at the dining room table, too. We all laugh and talk, and it feels good. I like it too, when the girl cousins, Vicky, and April, come over and we sit on the bed and talk. We're all the same age. I like that. Someone my own age to be a friend. It makes me miss my friends and Bella and Nini less.

I did look forward to the big Sunday dinners, where the parents are nice all day. I help cook and I even get enough food. Reminding me of Mother Ackley house where I always had enough to eat. I still make sure Junior's and Yasmin's have enough because I'm never sure.

Labor Day was the first holiday there. I can't believe we are celebrating a holiday like Labor Day. So, I wondered what it'd be like. We ended up having a big picnic in the park with everyone including some of Daddy Mark's family from Chicago. I barely remember celebrating any holidays before this. At the park, we divided up into teams and played kickball. I try my hardest to kick the ball as far as possible because I love to run, and I can run pretty fast. My goal is to make it all the way around the bases. I want to show them that I am good at something. Maybe I am going to be okay.

Before school starts, Daddy Mark takes us to Kmart in their yellow station wagon. Mama Betty is already there because it's where she works. We are going to buy brand new school clothes. I am thrilled that we don't have to get our clothes from the Salvation Army. Maybe the kids at my new school won't tease me. I got three pieces: two skirts and a pair of pants. Daddy Mark picks out the outfits. I don't want to wear skirts all the time, especially the long ones Daddy Mark chooses. And Mother Ackley made me wear dresses all the time because of her religion. So, I asked for pants instead, Daddy Mark says no and calls me a tomboy. Why wearing pants makes me a tomboy. I am just tired of dresses. I can't say that out loud. I don't know how he will react. Maybe whip me. Like what happens to Junior when he teases Shay or when Shay complains about Yasmin playing with her toys, the look in Mama Betty's eyes is like hate. She uses a belt to whoop them. So far, Daddy Mark doesn't hit them until told too. I want all the whooping's to stop, but there is nothing I can do. Through any good times, I know that someday there will be another whooping, and it erases any hope I start to feel.

I am going to start seventh grade in honors classes in math and English. I'm going to Iroquois Middle while Yasmin, Junior, and Shay will go to Alexander Elementary School a short distance away. I was worried at first about being away from them, but I have to go to school, so there is no choice. Because we live in a nice neighborhood, it's okay for them to go alone. Doug goes to Ottawa Hills High School. He leaves way earlier than the rest of us. He has a car to drive to school. Doug drops Daddy Mark off at first shift at Kelvinator, so he can keep the car. He is in his senior year, five years older than me, and he seems like a grownup even more when he is driving. He acts different, too. He doesn't wave or say anything before he drives away.

When we get to the end of the driveway, Shay, Yasmin and Junior turn to go in the other direction, and I have to walk six blocks by myself down Fisk Street. All the houses are nice with pretty green grass in the front yards and big backyards, which is new to me. The houses aren't old and rundown looking, and there are flowers and plants in front of the neat porches. There are only a couple of black families in the neighborhood besides Daddy Mark and Mama Betty. I never noticed until now, and it doesn't seem like it makes a difference; the neighbors are still nice to all of us. All the get-togethers are with family who drive over, not like at Grandmo's where everybody is just there.

As I get to the last two blocks, I catch up to a girl ahead of me, and she says we can walk together. Her name is Rennie, and she kind of looks like me. It seems like a good thing that I may have a friend. I have already decided that I'm not going to be bullied this time. Nobody at school is going to boss me around because I am going to be tough. Each morning, I looked forward to catching up to her so we could walk together. Her parents know the Carpenters. She is in some of my classes in seventh grade. Rennie is a new student, too, because she had been going to a private school in elementary school.

Rennie and I get in trouble because we talk too much. Mostly I am bored because my classes are too easy, except the honors classes. There is a white boy named Marcus Calloway. We are the smartest kids in our grade, so we team up for our group projects and we get to be the judge and lawyer when our class does a mock trial. We have a little friendly competition to see who is smarter because we are in three classes together. We both raise our hands whenever the teachers ask a question to see who will be picked and who will answer correctly. He's the first white boy I know, except for Vanessa's son. After my first kindergarten class in California, I have only gone to school with black kids, so this school is different. It shouldn't matter that he is white, but I have always been the smart one and I don't want that to change. It's okay in school to have white friends and to hang out with white boys, but not at home. Having a friend like Marcus made being smart feel okay, though. I always liked being smart, but now school is everything. When I don't have school, I go to the library. I love learning, but now I like that I feel special knowing things. It seems I am one of only a few black kids in the hardest classes.

Rennie and I are becoming best friends. I like to go over to her house because her family is nice to me. We get to go to Rennie's room when I spend the night there on the weekends. She has her own room, and it looks like a princess's room. She has a beautiful twin bed with a pink headboard. The room is white and pink, like my room with Yasmin and Shay, but she gets it all to herself and everything in there is nice. She has a special dresser to hold all her pretty jewelry. She has a door to the garage rooftop, so we can go outside to sit and see the stars. I think her life is heaven--she has a mom and dad and brothers who all love her and treat her like a princess. I wish I had her life. I tell Rennie how lucky she is and that I want to be like her.

We are a team, Rennie and Regina. Her mom is so nice to me. So, I didn't mind calling her Mama Doris. She tells everyone Rennie and I are best friends and points out how we look alike. I feel so happy and proud to be almost part of the family. Except for this one time, Rennie's mom even invited me to go shopping with them. I am happy to go to the mall because we only ever shop at Kmart. Rennie's mom buys her all the new clothes that she wants while I watch. I don't have money to buy anything for myself. The saleslady asks why I'm not getting anything. Rennie's mom says, "She's not my daughter." This feels like a blow to my heart. She told me to call her Mama Doris, but just like all the other mothers I was supposed to have, she wasn't my mom. I should have known better than to pretend I had a mom, even for a few minutes at JCPenney.

Sometimes when we are done with chores after Sunday dinner, Daddy Mark lets me go with Rennie and her cousin Jill to the Savoy to see movies. Jill is two years older than us, and she and Rennie always dress fancy. We get car horns blew a lot of the older men we pass on the way. It feels good to get attention, thinking someone thinks I look good. Or are they just blowing at Rennie and Jill? When we get to the movies, we see some of the other kids from school and meet up with kids from other schools. Going to the movies is one of the best parts of my week.

The first Christmas in what is still our foster home is awesome. We all got toys. I even got a typewriter for Christmas because Daddy Mark finds out I am learning to type. I am twelve and it is my second Christmas ever, after the one at Mother Ackley's when she gave me the children's bible. I didn't have any big expectations for Christmas, and I didn't even believe in Santa Claus. A white man giving me a present...right?

We have a big tree decorated with Christmas ornaments. The whole house has decorations. Mama Betty spent two days cooking dinner for all seven of us. She makes sweet potato pie, collard greens, a big ham, cornbread, and candied yams. We kids help, and she gives us directions, which is the most she has ever talked to me. It doesn't feel like we are getting any closer, but it makes me happy to be cooking this kind of food that I love.

After Christmas break, we go back to school. I'm still excited about the Christmas presents, but I'm also looking forward to my birthday. I had never celebrated my birthday before, but it made me feel special to have a day all to myself. There really weren't celebrations in my foster homes.

The second semester of seventh grade starts. I'm thinking I want to play a sport. I learned basketball tryouts are in gym class after school. It's intramural and I am chosen. We get put into teams. I know a couple of the girls on my team, and it's funny because there is another girl named Regina, and a girl named Gina. We made a good team, and practices were fun. I would feel so happy to be so popular even for an hour or two.

I'm still friends with Rennie, and I have two other friends named Taylor and Dana. One of the best parts of school is that nobody knows my history. Except Rennie, Taylor and Dana knows I'm a foster kid. I am keeping to my vow not to be a follower. There's a girl named Rhoda who was Rennie's best friend before I came. One day she takes my shoe from me in gym class while we are getting dressed. She throws it across the gym floor as we walk from the locker room to the gym. I told her to pick it up. She ignores me with a smirk. I told her again. No response. The third time I tell her, she says, "I ain't picking nothing up." Then she pushes me. Everyone gathers around. I know that if I don't stand up to this bully, everyone will pick on me for the rest of the year. She shoves me again, so I fight back. I am proud that I didn't just take it--I hit her and threw her to the floor. But the gym teacher comes to break us up and take us to the office. We get detention. I just take the time to do my homework, but I am scared about what Daddy Mark will do. Surprisingly, he doesn't seem to have a problem. He just says your grades better not be affected. I thought, whew. I've only got in a fight once in school and the foster parents didn't seem to care either.

The rest of school is great, though. Miss Darrow is my math teacher. She is wonderful. Me and another black girl are the only black students who are picked for Algebra, a new class for advanced students. It's the first time Algebra is offered to middle school students. I feel proud to be chosen, and the class was more challenging than most of my classes, but it is still fun to learn. Me and the other black girl sit in the back corner of the class. We talk sometimes, and the teacher shushes us.

Math is my favorite class, and home economics is second. I like learning to cook and sew. I don't know how I will use these skills, but it feels good to be able to do stuff for myself. My teacher is black--I've never had a teacher who wasn't white before. Miss Washington is my English teacher. She is also black. I don't love English, but I know I have to learn and memorize everything to get an A. I usually get my work done early. One time, Taylor and I talked after my work was done, and we got in trouble. Miss Washington tells Daddy Mark during a parent-teacher conference and this he grounds me for. The only place I really go is to Rennie's house anyway, but I'm happy when the grounding is over. Glad basketball was over, too.

Seeing that teachers could be black amazes me. I think I might want to be a teacher, too. I remember all the days I played 'school' and taught Junior and Yasmin. School is such a wonderful and safe place to be. I could stay in school all my life. I have friends, people to talk to, people who look like me. I understand how school, works, I think there's sort of an assigned order to kids. It depends on how much money their parents make. Rennie is at the top. Her parents must have a lot of money. She lives only one block away from East Grand Rapids, which I learned was a rich part of town. Daddy Mark and Mama Betty are okay, living a few blocks away from East

Grand Rapids, and maybe that transfers to me, but it's more important that I am friends with Rennie than where she lives.

Talking too much gets me in trouble again. School work is so easy that I always finish early and have to sit and wait for the other kids. Part of my grades include behavior, and I get a C on my report card for talking too much. Daddy Mark sees my report card and cusses me out. He says, "You are better than this. You are acting dumb." My feelings are so hurt that I cry, almost more than any other time. It is the first time I ever got a bad grade, but I don't feel bad until I see Daddy Mark's reaction. Nobody ever seemed to care about the good grades, so it is a surprise that somebody cares at all. I made a vow that I would never get a C again. I'll try to do better. Daddy Mark doesn't like me talking too much to Rennie anyways because I might tell her something about what happens at home. I get in trouble for that, too.

One of the best parts of the week is the skating nights. Every few weeks on a Friday night, the school paper would announce that it was Iroquois Middle School night at Woodland Skating. Rennie didn't skate, but I loved it, so I would meet other friends there. I learned to skate in Jackson when I was little. MLK Center had skating for twenty-five cents, and I got to go. In middle school, I got really good at skating--I can go backwards and skate dance. All the boys want to skate with me. I love the music and the dancing and the attention. Skating is one of the best things ever. My cousin Gigi taught me to skate when we were seven. "Stand up. You have to balance." I was so happy the first time I went around the whole thing without falling, and I still feel the same way when I am skating. I tell myself, "Keep going, keep going." And then I am lost in the music, black music, soul music. As I glide around the rink, I feel like I can go anywhere. I can escape.

When I go to Rennie's house, her mom asks me questions about where I come from. She knows Daddy Mark and Mama Betty, so she knows that we aren't their kids. She knows before Rennie. I tell Rennie a little about my life, and she tells her mom. When her mom asked, I admitted that my dad was in jail and my mom left to become a singer. That's how my dad always explained it. Rennie made a vow to help me find her. Her mom, though, told Daddy Mark what I had said. He cussed me out again. "You talk too much, telling people your business. You talk too much in school. If you keep doing that, I won't let you go see Rennie anymore." It reminded me of Grandmo. I can't believe that I let myself feel safe enough to forget what her beating taught me. I'll tell Rennie that I got in trouble. We keep telling each other secrets and we pinky swear we won't tell our parents. She tells me about her family, too. Her life isn't so bad, and I don't tell her about the worst things about mine. I still want to be a girl without a history in this new school.

Doug is supposed to graduate from high school. By the end of the year, Doug failed some classes, though he did graduate. He tells me he was a good student until his senior year. He says that his parents don't care about what grades he gets, so he doesn't care either. We go to the Gerald R. Ford auditorium (the city's Junior college). I am amazed at all the people in the gym and all of the kids in their caps and gowns. I think, one *day I'm going to be up there, hopefully in five years*. Doug had taken the test for the air force, and passed it, but they ended up rejecting him because he had broken a hip when he was little. He does gets money by babysitting his cousins. He says he is going to Key 5 Institute to learn about programming.

Since my 7th grade year of school is over, I start going to the library every day. It's okay to leave Yasmin and Junior. Yasmin plays with Shay and sometimes a girl across the street. Junior hangs around with Doug. I'm in the middle again, with nobody my age, just like at Mother Ackley's. Daddy Mark is the only one who talks to me. Daddy Mark sometimes takes us to Johnson Park. His cousins from Chicago come to visit in the summer, and that is the best time. Nobody is mean, they cook up a storm, and we get to do fun things. We even go on vacation. Down south to Houston to meet Daddy Mark's mother. I get to go with a cousin to Six Flags. That is the only time I have ever been to an amusement park. It was so fun. So many rides. I got on all the big ones. All that riding made me hungry. I had to go among the many food booths. They had cotton candy. I don't ever remember eating that before. I got a pink bag with the little money I had. And a corndog. I thought I would try it. It was good, too. We stayed until almost dark. I didn't want to leave, but we were to be picked up soon and were told to be at the entrance gate.

A few days after we got back from Houston, Daddy Mark showed me a paper. "Look, you went on the fastest ride in the country," he told me, pointing to an article in the paper about the roller coaster I was brave enough to ride. I am happy, and I know I will love amusement parks for the rest of my life. There are some good times here, and I try to pay attention to them and not worry too much about the bad times. Maybe I'll be okay like Granmo said.

Chapter 13

Blood and Water

"No death, no doom, no anguish can arouse the surpassing despair which flows from a loss of identity." — H.P. Lovecraft, The Dream-Quest of Unknown Kadath

When September comes, I feel anxious. It is over a year since we met the Carpenters, and we are supposed to be adopted today. I have known this day was coming for a month. The social worker and Daddy Mark sat us down to explain what was going to happen. They said we would get a new last name, Carpenter. Daddy Mark also told us that this would be a chance to change our first names, too. I took Yasmin and Junior to the pink bedroom. I told them that they couldn't change their first names because our dad had chosen our names, and they meant something. I told Yasmin that she was named after a movie star. I told Junior that he was Charles Lee after our daddy.

When I tell Daddy Mark that we aren't going to change our names, he says we can choose middle names if we want. I had seen a name on 'Wheel of Fortune' that I thought was beautiful, so I chose it, Elissa. Yasmin decides to choose Denise. Junior is keeping his first and middle name, but in the adoption, he is no longer Junior. We are supposed to stop calling him JUNIOR now. Our last name is no longer Moore. We are supposed to be Carpenter now.

It seems like I should feel relief. The adoption means that we weren't going to be sent to another home. Yasmin, Junior and I would be together until we grew up. I take solace in that. I still feel like I have lost my identity. I don't have the same last name as my daddy. I don't have any cousins anymore. I hugged Yasmin and Junior and told them we will always be together. I don't have any excuse now not to call Daddy Mark and Mama Betty my mom and dad, but I don't want to do it. It's easy not to say the word *mom* to Mama Betty because she never talks to me. But Daddy Mark expects me to call him Daddy.

Mama Betty always says, "Blood is thicker than water." I feel a division. Yasmin and Junior and I are on one side, and the rest of the family is on the other. When Yasmin and Shay get in a fight, I always stand behind Yasmin. She still gets beaten because Mama Betty is always on Shay's side. We are a family, and they are a family. When Yasmin, Junior, and I talk, I remind them that we are blood. I hug and kiss them. We tell each other that we love each other. We are all we have. We three are family always and forever.

I think one time Daddy Mark must have overheard me telling my sister and brother that we are family because at the dinner table one night, he says, "I didn't fuck for any of you." It is the first time I heard that word spoken aloud in this home, but I know what it means. I know he isn't our daddy. But of Doug or Shay. How can that be? I asked Doug that night in the basement what was that all about? He confides in me, now that we are friends. Doug tells me that Daddy Mark met his mom when he was three, when lived in Louisiana. She married Daddy Mark when Doug was six. And Shay was adopted when she was a little baby.

None of this makes me feel any better about being adopted. We have to do things with the rest of the family. We have to eat dinner with them and go on trips with them, but we are still our own little family. I am not angry anymore. Maybe just sad. But not the day I'm told by Daddy Mark that we get to go see my real daddy.

We are on a Greyhound bus going to Jackson. Yasmin and Junior and I are alone. We are the only kids all by ourselves on the bus. Daddy Mark has told us that when we get off the bus, our dad will be there to pick us up. We go through Lansing, the city that we met the Carpenters and which I saw on a map is pretty much halfway. I know now where the hundred miles from Jackson was, Grand Rapids exactly. I am in charge of keeping Yasmin and Junior safe and behaved. I have one on each side of me. We spend a lot of time looking out the windows. I tell them how lucky we are to get to see our daddy. Yasmin and Junior hadn't seen him since Frankie Mae's house. That is a long time, and they are so little. Junior mostly just remembers daddy going to jail and what he promised him to always do. Yasmin only remembers a little daddy always picking her up. We talked about daddy on the bus because I want to be sure they remember where we came from. I am still in shock because the social worker said he wasn't our father anymore. I didn't think I'd ever get to see him again until I was grown. It has already been two years for me.

When we got off the bus, Daddy and Vanessa were there. He drove his fancy cream colored Cadillac, just like he always drove. We all ran over to him and hugged him. I can't resist asking, "Do we get to stay with you?" He tells me no, but we get to visit him for a while. He is out of prison, and I am happy to see him without handcuffs, so he can actually hug me. He is wearing his cowboy outfit with a cowboy hat. We go right to Vanessa's house. There is a new swing set in the yard. We played with Vanessa's kids. Daddy puts Patty and Yasmin on his lap; they are both his little girls. In this family there is no division between blood and water. I like that Daddy's says that.

I stayed in the living room with Daddy when the little girls went out to play. Daddy starts by telling me to always love Jade. He then starts asking me questions about where we live. How are we being treated. I don't tell him about the whippings because I don't want him to get mad. And I don't want Daddy-Mark not to let us come back. I wish we could stay. They have room. But I know we can't. I am so happy to just see Daddy not in chains like before.

When the weekend is over, we get in Daddy's Cadillac to go back to the bus station. I have been so happy that I don't want to leave. I ask Daddy if we will be able to come back again. He says, "I hope so." Yasmin and Junior fall asleep on the bus ride back to Daddy Mark and Mama Betty's. I look out the window. It reminds me of the window on the train ride when *she* dropped us off. I call my daddy my real daddy. I must call the adopted dad, Daddy still, but I try not to. I think of him as Daddy Mark, never my real daddy. Though, Daddy nicknamed him Dear-Old-Dad. That made me laugh.

I am in eighth grade now. Going back to school is exciting. I hope Rennie and I are in more than one class together. Doug has dropped out of Key 5, and he is babysitting for money. Even though he lives at home, he seems like a real adult with a babysitting job. When I get a job, I am leaving. But first I must finish school.

When I started typing class halfway through the seventh grade, the address I had for Mama Baxter, *her* mother, suddenly made sense. The teacher stood at the front of the room with a long envelope. She drew a picture of it on the chalkboard and then demonstrated how to write out an address. She showed us how to type our own address in the upper left corner and the TO address in the center. Then she passed out envelopes and told us to copy what she had done on the board onto the envelopes. I didn't copy. Instead, I typed out Mama Baxter's address in the center. How did I know this address. I'd say it out loud sometimes so I wouldn't forget it. I then typed my address in what would be my last foster home and new adoptive home, though I didn't know it at the time, in the upper left corner. I wanted them to know where we were. I felt the only way was to write letters and mail them. No matter what.

Age 13

As Daddy Mark took on the role of father, even buying my first school picture since Simi Valley, he checked up on my schoolwork and found the envelope. "Where did you get those address?" he asked me, hovering over me. "I am not sure, but I think Mama Baxter, my mother's mother said I should always remember it," I said. "I'm going to send her a letter." "You'll need a stamp," he told me. The letter was sealed, so he couldn't know what it said, so he gave me a stamp. It was the first of many letters, I only got a response to that first letter, so I knew Mama Baxter knew where we was. I didn't know if she told *her*. I now have a connection, though I eventually realized they weren't coming for us, but I will continue to look for the rest of my life.

The letters say different things. I never tell Mother Baxter about the bad things that happen. I told her how Yasmin and Junior were growing. About what I am learning in school. I never ask about her daughter—who seems a stranger more than anything, someone I only referred to in my mind as *her*. In fact, even when I lived at Grandmo's nobody but me mentioned my mother at all. Not Grandmo, not my aunts, not my father, except to tell me that I should love *her* no matter what. Yasmin and Junior are too little to have any memory of her.

But somewhere deep down, I felt a connection to *her*. I know a place where *she* had been. When my cousins used to tease me because I didn't have a mother, I repeated the address in my mind, and I made up what I would say in a letter. When the kids at school asked why I didn't have a mother or called me an orphan, I remembered that there was a place that I could go to when I was a grownup and that I might find my mother there. Now that I could actually send mail there, I even thought that there might be a chance she was reading my letters. I wrote carefully, with my best handwriting and tried to make sure that I sounded smart and clever, like somebody that a grandmother would love, like somebody that a mother would want to keep with her and take care of the way I was taking care of Yasmin and Junior. I wrote like somebody who mattered to people, even though I felt like I didn't.

One time when Yasmin and Junior and I got to go to visit Daddy, he told me that he tried to keep us. He says that when he knew we were going into foster care he called Mama Baxter and asked her to tell the courts she was going to raise us. He told her she just had to pretend, and he would take us. She just had to make sure we didn't get into foster care because the courts were saying he wasn't our daddy. Mama Baxter wouldn't do it. Later Daddy tells me the word bastard--it's a kid whose mama isn't married to her daddy. Mama Baxter said she didn't want his bastard children. That's what the courts said we were, and that's why they took us away. Even though I know what she said, I keep writing letters. I'm not even mad because it doesn't seem possible that I could have had another life. It seems like everything that happened was because it was just supposed to be that way. I was not to be part of my real family. And it seems like nobody cares enough to turn the direction of my life or to stop it from continuing to be fake.

The only one who seems to care now is Doug. He listens to me now when I tell him about how I grew up. I feel important having somebody older than me tell me about things he doesn't say to anybody else. And he acts like he cares about my life and my feelings, something that I never expected. Daddy Mark seems to realize what is happening, but he doesn't stop anything. Daddy Mark one day comes to me and says that the social worker told him, "Be careful of Regina, she would like somebody Doug's age. She would be crushing on him." I don't know if the social worker really said that or if it is just a way for Daddy Mark to tell me that anything that happens is my fault; he believes like everybody else that I am fast. I feel ashamed about how I feel, how much I like Doug paying attention to me. Before anything happens, I feel guilty. It's almost like I know trouble is coming, but I just want to cling to this little bit of happiness, no matter what.

The year goes on with school, and getting by at home, and sitting in the basement talking with Doug. I don't talk to Mama Betty ever, and the only time we have together is when she presses my hair. Daddy Mark is even more controlling, and I am afraid of him, afraid he will get mad at me if I don't get all As. Christmas now that we are adopted is not as extravagant as the first year, but I had grown to expect nothing--and at least it was better than nothing. I asked Daddy Mark for a doll; I had never in my life had a doll to play with, but Daddy Mark must have thought I was too old. Yasmin, Junior, and I each got a paper bag of fruit and candy, one outfit and one gift. Yasmin and Junior feel bad watching Shay open all her toys, but I try to show them how fun their gifts are. I don't tell them blood is thicker than water, but that is what I think. Per Mama Betty.

Junior's favorite food is yams. One night, Daddy Mark asks him if he wanted yams at dinner, and Junior replies, "Are you crazy?" Of course, he wants yams. He thought Daddy Mark was kidding when he asked such an obvious question, we all did. Instead of laughing, Daddy Mark goes into a rage. We were already adopted, so the beatings had gotten worse, but this time he beats Junior with his fists for being a smart aleck.

Whenever Yasmin and Junior get a whipping, they go upstairs to their rooms. I can't stop the whooping's, but I can try to make them feel better. I follow them up and say, "I love you. We're going to get out of here one day. You're going to be okay." Even if we aren't getting whipped, we have to do the worst chores. In winter, Junior must shovel the snow, no matter how deep it is or how cold, even though he was only 10 when he started shoveling, and no adult will help him. I try to warm and console him when he comes in cold. I try to teach them and show them they can have fun. My favorite is still playing school. At least Yasmin and Junior never get in trouble about school. Maybe teaching them at home makes it easier for them. I like to think that I am helping them somehow. Every day, I tell Yasmin and Junior, "Remember, we are brother and sisters. How they love Doug and Shay, they'll never love us like that. I wish they could. I wish they would. When is someone going to love as they real kids? No one I think since *She* didn't.

I am fourteen during the summer of 1977, and there isn't really anything different, except Doug pays more attention to me. When he isn't going outside with Junior to play basketball or hanging out with his friends, Ryder and Frank, Doug and I hang out in the basement to watch tv. When his friends are around, he is a totally different person, teasing and picking on me or ignoring me like before. When we are alone, he treats me like a friend. I think I can endure the meanness for those nights when he makes me feel like he cares about me.

There's a record player downstairs, too, and Doug and I love a lot of the same music. I've always loved music since my real daddy used to play his albums, but I am starting to love the music Doug shares with me. Doug's favorites are the Commodores and Earth, Wind and Fire. They become my favorites, too. Earth, Wind and Fire have the best love songs. They are slow and rhythmic. Doug likes love songs, too, which I think might be a sign. Sometimes I get up and dance, swaying as though someone is holding me. It's almost like I can feel the love from those songs in my body. The best times are when Doug gets up and dances with me. It's a little scary when he first touches me because I know he is a man and I am just a girl, but after a while it feels nice. Other than hugging Yasmin and Junior, I never have people touch me, and there's a longing to feel connected and loved that I can't get away from. I get to stay up late with him because we are the oldest. Daddy Mark works the second shift, and I just have to be sure to be in bed before he gets home. Mama Betty is watching tv and talking to her sisters on the phone. She never cares what I do—if she notices.

Doug tells me secrets when we are talking together. One night--it was always at night when Doug doesn't have anything else to do--he explains why his dad picked us. Mama Betty didn't want us. She already had Doug, her son, and Shay who was adopted as an infant, but Daddy Mark had no biological kids. Daddy Mark thought that adopting three kids would get them money from the state. Michigan paid well—over $1000 in 1976 until the kids are eighteen or graduate from high school, whichever comes latest. The State of Michigan gives extra money to parents who do multi-kid adoption. We are considered special needs kids—black and older. I still try to think that maybe he wanted us because he wanted a family. Doug says Daddy Mark was told how good I was in school, and that might be why he wanted us. That's what made Daddy Mark's thing with me, that I would never fail in school. I'm not even allowed to get a C.

I'm supposed to be a good student and be good at other things, so I decided to go out again for the intramural basketball team. I love basketball, and I go to all the boys' games when they are at home, but I don't think I can be good enough to play on the girls' team. The idea of playing against other teams in our school, with kids who I go to school with and know, makes me feel safer. For weeks I was so happy to stay after school. To be part of something. To be known as someone, not a foster child, a child without parents. At the end of the season, we emerged as the school champions, and we all got a certificate and had our team picture taken for the yearbook. Daddy Mark and Mama Betty don't really pay attention to this--they don't come to the games or the awards ceremony, but I am just happy that I get to stay after school to do something fun.

I am finished with eighth grade, and I plan to spend another summer going to the library and getting ready for high school. I hope I can win the award for reading the most books at Ottawa Hills Library like I did last year. I graduated middle school with a high-grade point average, and I knew high school was going to be a great new adventure. Even though my intramural basketball team won the championship in middle school, I was going to concentrate on my studies in high school.

Rennie is still my best friend, but I have other friends, too, which makes me feel so lucky. Plus, we have aunts and uncles and cousins from Mama Betty's family--most of Daddy Mark's family lives in other states. Sometimes I hang out with

Velma, who is the same age as me. She is Mama Betty's sister's child. Daddy Mark and Johnny, who is Velma's father, start a CB Radio Club with a bunch of men they know, all around the same age. They take me and Velma to parties where we are told to dance with the men, even though they look old to me. I love to dance and think it's fun anyway. Daddy Mark and Ronnie make money by selling drinks, so they want to keep the men there as long as possible. Daddy Mark is nice and funny around adults, but all the kids are afraid of him like I am.

I don't like the way they smell, like liquor. At first it is fun, but it starts to feel weird having all these old men hanging around me. I don't want to stop because Velma and I are becoming friends, and I get to spend the night at her house sometimes. It feels good to have a cousin and to have Daddy Mark need me for something--maybe I am special and good. I love the music and dancing, and I'm really happy if I just pay attention to that and don't think about the men. Even so, I tell Velma how weird it feels. She tells me that if you do things with these men, they will buy you stuff. I smile when I'm dancing, but I don't really know what I would do to make the men buy me things. When men or boys did things to me in the past, I never got anything. This is different because Daddy Mark is making me do it, so it must be okay.

I just love to dance so Daddy Mark puts me in a step club. A woman named Shelia started the club, and she teaches young girls how to step. Shelia tells us that it is an African tradition and that we should use our bodies like instruments and mark the beats with footsteps and hand claps. There are about a dozen girls in the class, and there is something amazing about being part of a group, all moving together, all making music with our bodies. We do a combination of dance, clapping, and spoken word. It is supposed to help us be proud to be black. I feel proud, and I really love the step club.

Step club gives me more confidence about my dancing. So, a fellow teen named Jerry Newman, and I entered a dance contest. Since I love R&B and disco it was easy to dance to The Spinners, Cameo, and Earth, Wind and Fire. I can feel the music move through my body and the rhythm takes over. I feel free and happy, and dancing with Jerry, who is a year older than me and super popular, makes me feel special. Jerry is tall and dark like Doug. He has a 'fro like Doug, too. I can't believe he asked me to dance with him in the contest. Me, he picked me. Does that take away my nerves and let me just dance without fear? I think so because I don't even realize all the people watching us and just focus on the music and the movement.

Dancing is a time when my body takes over and I can just be myself. My mind stops thinking and worrying. The rhythm takes over and I am suddenly bigger and better than my regular self. All of life's problems float away on the music and the lyrics shape my emotions so I feel the joy or the love that the singer describes. I become one with the music and the people dancing with me. Somehow, Jerry and I have a connection, and our bodies move together to the music like people on tv. Everything feels perfect. And we won! Jerry and I hugged, and everyone congratulated us. My heart is beating so fast, and I can't help but smile and laugh because I feel so good.

Chapter 14

Make You a Woman

"I am not ashamed of what I am and that I have curves and I am big. I like my body." —Alicia Keys

Now that Doug is treating me like a friend, I am thinking about boys in a new way. Maybe Daddy Mark notices this because he seems to start talking to me differently. He is crude sometimes and he tells me bad things about girls who want attention from men, even though he keeps taking me to the CB Club. One night when we are all at the table--we always eat dinner together--he says, "When you think you want a boy, I'll give you a pickle." I don't even want to understand what he is talking about. Why would I eat a pickle if I had a crush on a boy? The way he says it, though, makes me think it's something bad, sort of like when the kids at school tease me because my name is Regina, and it sounds like vagina. It's something to do with doing the nasty, but I don't have anybody to explain that to me. The only thing I know about my vagina is that it is the place between my legs, and it is bad because that is where Frankie Mae said blood comes out from. I never even say that word. I'm afraid to ask more about all those private things, and don't know who to ask anyway. Now I think Doug and Mama Betty and all the kids are staring at me, so I feel embarrassed.

Daddy Mark also tells me about his sister Bianca. She got pregnant as a teenager, and her father got really mad at her and beat her, trying to get the baby out. I wonder what she did to get pregnant. Why was it her fault? Daddy Mark makes it sound like a bad thing, but I don't know why he is telling me. I don't know how I could have a baby, anyway. I'm too young.

One night when I was going up to my bedroom to read, I passed Doug on the steps. He looks at me and says, "I'm going to make you a woman." He makes a gesture with his hands, forming a circle with his finger and thumb and thrusting his finger into the hole. I don't know what that means, but he smiles and that makes it seem like a good thing. Doug's nineteen and I am only fourteen. It never occurs to me that I have a choice.

Age 14

"Make me a woman?" I say, and I feel a little excited. I am starting to have a crush on Doug. Is it possible that he could feel the same way about me? I have tried not to think about what my cousins and Grandpa Carpenter did to me, blocked it out any way I can, but now I start to realize what Doug means. This is something that a husband and wife do together, and it means they love each other. Maybe Doug loves me. Just thinking that makes me feel like I might have a place in the world after all. But I also realized something else. He is a man, and he is going to do what men do. He is going to touch me where it hurts, where they hurt me. Instead of being excited I started feeling scared. I don't know how I will live through this, and I know it is my job to make Doug happy, so he will love me and talk to me again and make me feel important. I have to figure out a way to be ready when he wants me. I tell myself I'll be ok. I like him so much so doing this is ok?

The next night, when Doug and I are in the basement and everybody has gone to bed, Doug tells me what to do. "Lay down on the couch. I'll teach you the facts of life." I do it. He pulls up my nightgown and pulls off my panties. He unzips his pants and tells me to spread my legs. When he pushes into me, I feel the pain again, but it isn't as bad as when 'Grandpa' tried. I feel his jeans and his belt rubbing against my belly and thighs.

He is so much bigger than me. It only lasts a couple of minutes, and I focus on the ceiling and tell myself that this is going to make me a woman, just like Doug wants. He knows what I told him about Grandpa Carpenter, but this must be different. Doug has a towel ready, and I feel him jerk out of me and see him wrap his private in the towel.

"It is over?" I ask. He doesn't say anything to me and just nods. So, I pull on my panties and pull down my nightgown. Doug still doesn't say anything to me. We sit there and watch tv like it is a regular night. I think I must have done it wrong because Doug won't talk to me. After a while, I just go up to bed. Doug barely looks at me in the morning and a few days go by before he says something to me. Though, we keep watching tv at night, just like normal.

Then one night, Doug turns to me and tells me to lie down on the couch. I know what he wants, so I pull off my panties and wait for it to be over. This happens a few more times when nobody is around. I tell myself that it is good. Doug likes me, and I am becoming a woman. The summer goes on like this until it is time for vacation. We are going to Houston to visit Daddy Mark's family.

The very long drive again. It's not so bad as I play 'how far we are game' with myself. Since I learned how to count miles and read all the green info signs. I love reading billboards too. In Houston, I am invited to stay with Doug's cousin Jamie and her brother Coolie. Jamie is seventeen and Coolie is twenty, so they have their own apartment. It will be more fun for me to stay there, and there isn't a lot of room for me at Daddy Mark's mother's house, so a few nights at their apartment will be better than spending the whole week in the crowded house. Even though we aren't old enough, Jamie says we can get into a bar, and it will be really fun. There will be dancing. I love to dance, so I go with her--plus if I don't, I'll have to stay in their apartment by myself.

At first, it is a lot of fun. Jamie and I went out to the dance floor. Men keep coming over and asking us to dance. It feels thrilling to be in this grownup world. I think that maybe I am a woman now, like Doug said. Jamie finds a man she likes and disappears. I am alone on the dance floor with a bunch of men who keep trying to grab me and grope me. The music is loud, and the lights are flashing, and I feel like everything is closing in on me. I started to get scared, so I went to look for Jamie. She isn't anywhere I can see, so I go outside into the parking lot. We had walked there, but I know sometimes people went outside to get cooled off. Jamie is there and I tell her that I am scared and want to go home. She laughs at me and says she is having fun and isn't ready to leave. Coolie is there too, and he comes over to comfort me. It is such a relief to have someone I know, even if only for a day. I tell him what is happening. "I'm scared and I want to go," I say.

Coolie tells me that it's okay; he will walk me home. When we get back to their place, I thank Coolie for being so nice and tell him, "I'm going to go to bed until Jamie gets home."

"I'll take you up there," Coolie says. He is acting like a big brother who wants to take care of me. I haven't spent any time with Coolie until this night because he is a grownup. The only other time a man has been nice to me like this is when Doug talks to me in the basement. Coolie walks me upstairs to the bedroom where I am sleeping in one of Jamie's twin beds.

"I took you away from all of those men," Coolie says.

"Thank you," I say. I started thinking when Daddy Mark took me to the CB Club to dance, it wasn't like that-- those men weren't supposed to touch us. Coolie starts to take my clothes off. I don't understand what he is doing, so I say, "Stop please."

"You're going to be fine," he says in a soothing voice as he pushes me onto the bed. When he gets on top of me, I realize that he wants to do the same thing that Doug does, and those other men, if they had a chance, wanted to do the same thing. I lie there and wait until it is over. It has been two weeks since Doug started doing this to me, and at least it doesn't hurt this time. But it hurts my heart because I think I left all those men at the bar and still ended up with this man. I lay under Coolie crying silently until it's over.

Coolie doesn't pull out like Doug does. I feel wet down there, so when Coolie gets up and comes back with a towel to start wiping me, I think he is being nice. Plus, he talks to me afterward, not like Doug. I think that maybe I did it better this time and that is why Coolie still likes me. Before Jamie gets home, Coolie gets up and says to me, "You keep this between us." I know I am not going to say anything. What is there to say, and who is there to tell? Coolie is Daddy Mark's nephew, and I already know that blood is thicker than water. Even Jamie won't believe me, and if I tell anyone, I might get in trouble for being fast. I know men can do whatever they want, and I am supposed to let them have my body if that is what they want. But if I do that, I am the bad one. At least he was nice; he even wiped the tears from my eyes.

Even if he is nice, it reminds me of what Grandpa Carpenter did, and I know that I am never safe.

Nothing in life is ever safe. That is something I know for sure. What is it about me that makes men want to hurt me? Nobody has ever told me what men and women do together, but I am learning from experience that it must be bad and that somehow it is my fault. Daddy Mark has told me that I have a Coca-Cola body, but I don't know what that means, other than that men will want it, and it's my fault. I wonder if men have parts of their bodies that are their fault, but I've never looked at a naked man, so I don't know what they have that makes them the way they are.

The next morning, Coolie asks me to braid his hair. I sit on the couch, and he sits on the floor between my legs, and I braid his hair. Daddy Mark comes to pick me up, so I spend the rest of the vacation at his mother's house. It is very small and dirty, like a shack that I read about in some of my books. I am relieved when we are ready to drive home. I sit in the backseat with Yasmin and Junior, and even though I haven't seen them very much, I can't make myself talk to them on the long ride back. I am glad summer's nearly over.

By the end of summer, I try to forget about Coolie. I am going to have a good year this year, no matter what. Going to high school is exciting because I have friends; there are four of us who hang out together and I feel what it is like to belong. One of the girls is Teresa, who lives down the block from us now. I also get to go to the same school that Doug went to. Ottawa Hills High School had just been built before when he started--and now here I am. I love my social studies and geometry classes, and I take two electives--one of them is public speaking because I think someday, I am going to be a person who is going to make speeches. I am the only ninth grader in the class. Being with smart kids makes me feel confident and happy. I might be able to forget what happened this summer.

Ottawa Hills high school is in a nice area, so there aren't a lot of us black kids. None of the white kids in my classes become my friends. Mostly they ignore me. There is just one other black kid in my geometry class, a boy who is a Junior. His name is William, and we sit together and talk a little in class. He is shy, but really nice. I don't pay attention to the other kids in the class. Just like in elementary school, I mostly care that the teachers like me and think I'm smart. Rennie teases me sometimes—in a friendly way.

All of my advanced classes are with juniors and seniors, but I have typing with Rennie, and we're closer than ever. Rennie hates typing. Sometimes we skip class when her boyfriend drives us home early. Rennie has a lot more friends in her classes, so her friends become my friends. She is popular and fun. We just hang out at her house after school and listen to music. I tried a cigarette, but I didn't like it. I don't like the alcohol they drink either. Smoking and drinking are nasty. Remembering the time my dad held a rifle on me, I can't ignore what men do when they drink. But it's nice to feel like a normal kid. Nobody but Rennie knows about me. I am not a foster child or an adopted kid--I'm one of the cool people.

The only class I have in high school with a lot of kids that look like me is in Gym. That class is segregated, though not on purpose. White kids know how to swim, black kids don't. We hover at the shallow end, and even when the teacher tries to get us in the water, we just stand there, not knowing what to do. The only lesson he gives us is how to tread water. Nobody wants to get into the pool to try. Eventually the teacher gives up and only pays attention to the white kids. I had been so excited that I was going to learn to swim that I disliked standing there segregated. Us black girls are afraid to get our hair wet. Most black girls must have their hair straightened and we all know that if it gets wet in the pool, our hair will go frizzy. If that happens, you will get teased and there goes the rest of your day.

I decide I don't care, so one morning, I walk over to the deep end with the white kids and jump in. After I sink to the bottom, I remember that one lesson, how to tread water, and though I'm in fear of drowning I'm forced to become a fast learner. I can see the faces of the teacher and students around the pool, but nobody reacts--they just watch me as I do my best to keep from drowning until I make it above and tread to the side to hold on to something, anything. I hurried back to the shallow end, to where I belong with the non-swimmers.

Chapter 15

How Could You Leave Us?

"Abandonment doesn't have the sharp but dissipating sting of a slap. It's like a punch to the gut, bruising your skin and driving the precious air from your body."
— Tayari Jones, Silver Sparrow

When school gets out for the summer, I buy a bike with money I saved from babysitting. Doug drives all the time, and sometimes he drives me places, like taking me to get a wet burrito at night after everybody else is asleep. During this time, he teaches me how to drive. I like the feeling of freedom. I wonder if I will ever have a car to drive. He takes me to the Kmart where Mama Betty works, so I can buy my bike. Doug helps me pick it out. It's not like the bike I had at Mother Ackley's. It's yellow and green, and brand new. It's mine. I don't have to leave it if I go, and Daddy Mark can't tell me where I can ride my bike to as I'm fifteen, not ten. The bike is going to mean freedom, at least a little.

Daddy calls us. He doesn't call often because long distances are expensive. It's a big deal, so Yasmin and Junior and I rush to the phone to talk to him. Nobody at our house gets long distance calls very often, except when Daddy Mark talks to his sisters in Houston, but we all know that every minute costs money; it's expensive. My daddy taught me about calling collect, just in case there is an emergency, but I have never done that.

Daddy is excited, more excited than I have ever heard of him. He says, "Regina, I just heard your mama on the radio. She has an album. It came out a while ago, but this is the first I heard of it." I don't know if my daddy is excited because he really cares about *her* or if it's because he always tells me I have to love *her* no matter what, and this might be a way to make me love *her* and understand why *she* left us. As though everything we have been through might be okay because *she* got what *she* wanted. I must remind myself that Daddy doesn't know everything I have been through. The rest of the conversation is drowned out in my thinking. *I get to see her*

111

picture. I get to hear her voice. Daddy always told me that we moved to Hollywood in the first place because *she* wanted to be a singer. I believed that *she* left us so *she* could be a singer. All those times I thought, watched for *her* on tv with Bella and Nini in fifth and sixth grade. I never knew if they believed me, but now I have proof. It's too late for them, but I know that I have to see her album. I rushed to tell Rennie, and she is excited, too.

Rennie comes with me to Believe in Music on Fulton Street. We took the bus because Rennie doesn't ride a bike. I'm so excited and can't stop talking about it the whole ride over. We got off the bus and walked into the store. Believe in Music is a small corner shop. It's crowded with racks of records. We walk to the back and circle down the aisle to the R&B section. I love music; and have since my daddy played songs for me, and now that I know how much Doug loves music, it's even more important to me. This is one of the few times that I think of *her* as my mama. My mama has an album. It makes me feel proud.

I riffle through the albums and find the M's. *She* goes by Jade Moore. I see *her* name, my old name, on an album cover and there *she* is. Rennie peers over my shoulder and doesn't say anything. There is a picture of somebody I don't remember. I think about the woman I saw riding away in the back of the yellow cab, when I grabbed Junior's hand to make sure he was safe, the candy that had been a special treat worth nothing. Since I was little, I have always thought that all big women with little heads were great singers. I always notice in church that the women who sing with the most powerful and beautiful voices are big. I look at the album cover and wonder if this woman sang to me when I was a baby. Is that where I got my ideas about women who sing?

Jade is big and wears a black and white dress. *She's* pretty, but *her* skin is dark, much darker than mine and darker than I remember. The thing that surprises me most is how heavy Jade is. Even when I was five, *she* always talked about how important it was to look like a model. All the women my daddy had in California looked like they were fancy ladies. Vanessa was always pretty and dressed really nice, but Frankie Mae and Grandmo were big women; maybe that is what my daddy really likes. The woman on the album cover isn't that fancy. *Her* hair is like mine--a big fluffy afro. I am known at school for my thick, heavy hair, and now I can see where I got it from. Is there a connection here? I try to feel it. Daddy said it was her, but I don't even remember this woman. Maybe I don't know what she looked like, what she was like, at all. It has been ten years. I don't have enough money to buy the album. Looking at it has to be enough, but I am heartbroken.

It's the beginning of summer. And I am now fifteen and old enough to get a job. I applied and got a job scooping at Baskin Robbins Ice Cream parlor. I ride my 10-speed the two miles through the infamous Franklin Park, the only black neighborhood park in Grand Rapids, to the ice cream store where I am proud to make $1.70 an hour. When I get a raise of a nickel of an hour, I am thrilled. This is the best job ever. Riding my bike there makes me feel so much freedom. And then I get to the ice cream store and put on the hat—that makes me official. I make friends there with the other employees, and I love serving the customers. There's one mother with five or six boys, and she brings them every Sunday after church. I think it is so nice, and the boys are cute. The older two brothers are famous—their name is DeBarge, and their songs play on the radio all the time. All the customers are so nice. And best of all, I love ice cream. Sometimes when it's slow, the employees taste the different flavors with those little pink spoons. Every one of them is amazing. It's so much fun to have a job. And I love ice cream.

I started dating Doug's friend Ryder. Doug keeps having sex with me at night, but I don't have sex with Ryder. I remember at Rennie's someone had said once you can't have sex with two boyfriends. Because if you get pregnant you won't know who the father is. I tell myself I'm not going to have a baby. Doug told me that he pulls out to make sure I don't. Ryder kisses me on the mouth. Doug never kissed me. Ryder asks to go further but I say no. He surprisingly doesn't try anything. No pressure. Did he respect my wishes? I am not used to that. Or I think is he afraid of Daddy Mark? One time when we are late for curfew, Daddy Mark yells at me, and it's the first time I have ever been called a bitch. Hitting me is one thing but yelling at me and calling me a bitch is even worse. I have soft feelings, and words hurt more than hitting. Being

called a bitch feels like I am worth *less* than a female dog.
Ryder felt so bad. We were never late again.

I started the summer reading library books, hopefully,
earning the award for reading the most books again. I also get
to go with Rennie to her family reunion. It was weird seeing a
big family all in the same place. Everyone was very nice and
kept saying how Rennie and I looked alike.

As every July, when Daddy Mark says we are going to
Houston, I don't want to go again, so I say I have to work at
my job. He says it's okay for me to stay home. I am so
relieved.

It has been a year since Doug started having sex with
me in secret. Now that we are home alone, he feels safer. He
stops pulling out, he stops being quiet. After he is done, he tells
me he is sorry. He shouldn't be doing this, and he'll never do it
again. I try to remember that I am happy because he needs me,
and I am doing what I am supposed to do, even if we have to
keep it a secret from Daddy Mark and Mama Betty, from
everyone really. I am a woman now, though, so that makes me
feel proud and happy. It doesn't feel good when he pushes
himself into me, but I don't think about that; I think about good
things and try to get through it. I have a crush on Doug, so I tell
myself that I should be happy that I am making him happy.

When Doug apologizes, I'm worried that I might be
doing it wrong. Maybe he is rejecting me when he says he
won't do it again. I wish I had somebody to love me, somebody
besides Yasmin and Junior because they have to love me. At
least I have my friends.

I finally told Rennie what was happening, thinking
maybe she would be happy for me. The look on her face tells
me something is wrong. "You could get pregnant," she tells
me.

"No, Doug says he is pulling out, so I won't get
pregnant." I don't say that he doesn't do that every time now
that we are alone.

"That doesn't work," Rennie says. This makes me
worried, but I don't know what I can do about it. Doug is in
charge; he is twenty and I just turned fifteen and a half. He
must know more than Rennie. But what if Rennie is right? I

think about it and tell myself, "Good, if I have a baby, then I'll have somebody to love me."

Doug doesn't try to stop me from dating Ryder. He says it's a good cover for what we are doing at night. He says that I should be able to have a friend, even though he should always be my number one.

We still get to go to see my daddy sometimes. I found out that it is because my daddy is paying Daddy Mark regularly. That makes sense because I couldn't understand why Daddy Mark was doing it at first, mean as he can be. I tell my daddy what Doug told me in the basement. The State of Michigan is paying Daddy Mark and Mama Betty to keep us. Daddy seems upset. Daddy Mark always said, "Money talks." I think Daddy believes this too. He tells me to check the mail to find out how much money Daddy Mark and Mama Betty are getting for us. He says that when the mail comes on a certain day of the month, I should check the trash--there will be check stubs that will tell me the amount.

I'm the one who gets the mail, so it's easy for me to see when envelopes from the state come. Daddy is right; there are check stubs in the trash after that. Three of them, for over $378 each. That's over $1000 a month for me, Yasmin, and Junior. On our next visit, I told Daddy what I found. I can see he is mad, but he doesn't say anything. The next time we are due to go to visit, I call Daddy, and he says he is ready to pick us up at the bus station as soon as we get there.

When it's time to go, I ask Daddy Mark if he's going to drop us off.

"Fuck no. You ain't going". Does he know I know about the checks that I get, that I told my daddy? "You'll never see your daddy again." Fear comes over my whole body, like a tingling that starts at the top of my head and seeps into every limb. I had seen Daddy Mark beat my brother brutally and know what he might do when he is angry. I realize my dad must have said something to him, and I am in trouble. I don't move, and I stare into Daddy Mark's eyes. It's almost a dare, and I can't believe this is me standing up to him. Before I can think, words come out of my mouth.

"I'll see my dad when I'm eighteen." Even though Daddy Mark is scary, I never believed he would beat me, being a girl. The punch in the face comes so quickly and brutally that I don't even realize it happened until the pain sends a shock wave through me, throwing me backwards onto the couch. I realize this is going to be really bad as I take punch after punch. Daddy Mark is so big and strong, but then he must get tired of punching, so he kicks me. I try to shuffle away, crying and unable to scream, but he keeps kicking. I can taste the blood in my mouth and anger starts to take over. I realize this will not end until I fight back. I had barely ever talked back to an adult, let alone fight back.

I remember something I saw on tv that if you hit a man between the legs, it will hurt him. I force myself to stand and take aim while Daddy Mark goes to punch me again. I kick the hardest I can and see Daddy Mark bend over in pain. He stopped hitting me, but I am even more scared now. I run as fast as I can to my bedroom and block the door. As I'm going, I see that Doug was watching the whole time, and the front door is open, so I wonder who else has seen.

When my door handle jiggles, I have another jolt of fear. It's Mama Betty. She calls through the door, "Regina, you shouldn't have said nothing." She doesn't try to comfort me or see if I'm okay. I can feel the cuts on my face, but I'm too afraid to go to the bathroom to get a tissue and clean up. I pick a sock from my drawer and blot the flow of blood. I sink to my bed and hold the sock pressed against my face, catching the tears that I cannot stop. My face is swollen and hot. I can't believe that I've been punched in the face. It is just like on tv when men fight. I can feel my nose pulsing with pain and feel my face swelling up. My body is feeling nothing but pain. I am crying, not only because it hurts, but because I know I will never see my daddy again or at least for a long time. I vow to myself that on my eighteenth birthday, I will be in Jackson, Michigan, with my father again.

From the time my Grandmo had tied me to a pole to beat me for telling the teacher that I didn't have food, I had learned not to tell another adult what goes on in your home. Even if is true. Talking back to Daddy Mark had been the first time I had done that, and I know now that I should never open my mouth again. I am not allowed to have contact with Daddy anymore. But I continue to send letters to him because I can buy my own stamps.

Chapter 16

Baby on Board

"Only 40 percent of teen mothers finish high school. Fewer than 2 percent finish college by age 30."
https://www.ncsl.org/research/health/teen-pregTrina-affects-graduation-rates-postcard.aspx

In tenth grade Honors English class my teacher makes us write our life stories. After I turn in the assignment, the teacher asks to talk to me. This is when I find out my story is different from everybody else. Mr. Hoyt asks me if the story I wrote is true. I say yes, wondering what's the big deal. Everybody has their story. He asks if I ever thought about writing it down for a magazine article. I don't really understand what he wants. Does that mean telling people about my life? Will I go back to being the girl whose mother abandoned her? I am going to think about it, but I don't get a chance to decide.

While I'm at work at Baskin Robbins the smell of the ice cream is making me feel queasy. Until now, ice cream was one of my favorite foods, and all of us at work use the little tasting spoons to try the new flavors when we aren't busy. Pralines and Cream is my favorite flavor, but it doesn't taste good anymore. When I smell ice cream, I hate the feeling that my stomach turning and curling so much that I throw up sometimes. It gets so bad that I have to quit my job, which makes me really sad because ice cream is the best food ever and I loved my job so much until now.

It feels like I haven't had my period in a while. I remember what Rennie told me about maybe getting pregnant. I can't believe that it could really happen to me. Doug told me that pulling out keeps me from getting pregnant. But sometimes I ended up wet afterwards. I think that's when he didn't pull out. I'm not sure who to believe or what to do. I have heard girls at school talking about Planned Parenthood, so I looked up the address in the phone book. One day after school, instead of going to Rennie's, I got on the city bus to Cherry Street where the clinic is. As I am walking in, Velma is walking out. She smiles and points at me but doesn't say anything. I smile at her, too, but understand we aren't going to talk--we'll talk on the phone later. I don't know what to expect, but the waiting room is very nice. There are other teenage girls in there and a lot of reading materials. I take as many pamphlets as I can before I go into the room with the doctor. He examines me and has me pee in a cup. I have to wait for the results. It seems like hours. However, it was less than an hour. The nurse calls me into the room. Your test came back positive. You are pregnant, Regina. I'm stunned. Not sure what to think.

The first person I want to tell is Velma. So, I called her right away. She says we should spend the night the next day, and I ask Daddy Mark. He says it's okay since it's the weekend. When I go over, Velma and I sit in her bedroom together. She tells me she is pregnant, and I tell her I am, too. We laugh because even though we are so close, neither one of us told that we were having sex. I didn't because of Doug. Even I know he would be in big trouble if anybody found out. We compare due dates and find out our babies are coming nine days apart. That means that even though we are fifteen now, we'll be sixteen when our babies are born because our birthdays are only nine days apart. Deep down, I am afraid, but with Velma, I only talk about the good stuff. We are giddy and excited about our babies.

After the weekend, though, I have to go back home and tell Doug. I hope he will be happy; then not only will I have a baby who loves me, but maybe we can be a family. When I tell him, he just says, "Oh, shit." It isn't the response I wanted but it makes sense. Doug always said he wasn't going to make me pregnant, so he must not have wanted it. "You need to get an abortion."

"I can't do that," I say. I'm scared, but I know for sure I'm not getting any abortion. I know that meant killing the baby.

"You have to tell Daddy then," he says. I can see the fear in his eyes, and it makes me feel more afraid. I was already thinking about the beating that Daddy Mark gave me over the summer. It could be just like Daddy Mark told me about when his sister got pregnant, and his dad tried to beat it out of her. No matter what, I want my baby, so I am going to have to face him and be ready to fight back.

On Monday, I tell everyone I am too sick to go to school. I get to stay home. Everyone is at school, and Doug is at work, so when Mama Betty goes to work, I go to talk to Daddy Mark. He is in the kitchen cooking breakfast. I stand out of his reach and take a breath.

"Daddy, I have to tell you something". After a long pause, I say, I'm pregnant." My heart is beating like crazy and I'm so scared, but I know I must tell the truth.

"What?" Daddy Mark turns and looks at me. "By whom?"

"Doug."

"Your brother Doug?" After he asks, I have another thought. Like Mama Betty always says, blood is thicker than water. I am the adopted one, and this baby will be their blood. Can they take the baby away from me and send me away? This is another fear I will have to live with for the next seven months. I'm tempted to tell him that Velma is pregnant, too, hoping it will help me somehow. I don't, though, because I don't know if she has told her mama yet.

"Yes," I tell him. Daddy Mark is absolutely still for a moment. He doesn't say anything. Then he takes the pan off the stove, gets his keys, and leaves. That evening at dinner, I expected him to say something to me, but he didn't. He acts like I am not even there. Mama Betty never said anything to me anyway, so I don't know if he has told her yet. I go to bed as soon after dinner as possible.

The next night, I followed Doug to the basement, and I asked him if they had spoken to him yet. What did they say?

Doug tells me they asked him, "Were you her first? Is the baby yours?" He tells me that he said, "That's what she told me." Is he really doubting me, or is he just scared? Is he putting doubt in their minds? I expected them to question Doug, but I am hurt that Doug wasn't honest. He should have tried to convince them that the baby is his and that he was my first and only except for rape by Coolie last summer. I go to my room and cry, but this time, I think, I am not alone. From now on, my job is to protect and keep my baby. I don't know how to do that, but I will learn.

Chapter 17

Park School

"And when you look into her eyes, you won't believe the way she's always paying for a debt she never owes." — *Wildflower* **lyrics by Lisa Fischer**

"Your life is over." I hear those words from everybody I come across. Daddy Mark says it all the time. Nobody says that to Doug, now twenty. He has a part-time job, now, and everybody acts like it's a big deal. He spends all his money on new clothes, though, so he still stays at home. I think he doesn't want any responsibility, so he is willing to listen to Daddy Mark and Mama Betty. But I know I must take responsibility for everything so I can make sure my baby is safe and taken care of all the time.

I'm afraid to talk to the counselor at my school, but I have to. She is a black lady, and she doesn't feel like such a stranger because she knows Doug's family from church. I haven't been to her office yet because I have never been in trouble at school before, but I have no choice. I go into Mrs. Brown's office and sit across from her at her desk. She takes out my school file. As she turns through the pages, I see pictures of myself. I knew they took school pictures every year, but I had never seen them before. There had never been anybody interested enough to buy the packages that other parents bought for their children.

"Can I see those?" I ask. "I've never seen pictures of myself when I was little. Nobody ever bought my school pictures." She looks surprised, but she turns the file around on her desk so I can see. I lean in. As I look at myself, I feel a rush of sadness. It is so lonely knowing that I never had a mom or dad who would want those pictures. I have long hair and braids in most of the pictures. In a lot of the pictures my hair wasn't combed.

"So, Regina, what can we do today?" Mrs. Brown asks.

I don't want to say the words. School has been my sanctuary, the place where I am good and wanted. How can I give that up? I take a deep breath, knowing at least that she won't hit me. "I'm pregnant." I stop there, somehow knowing

that I can never tell anyone that Doug is the father. I don't
know about laws, but I do feel that other people will think this
isn't right because everyone thinks he is my brother. Doug had
warned me not to tell. He's the one who told me to tell
everyone it was Ryder. Then I was supposed to tell Ryder that
somebody in Jackson got me pregnant when I got to visit my
daddy. How could I say something bad happened the last time I
was allowed to see my daddy? I just don't say anything to the
counselor, and she doesn't ask.

"I think it would be a good idea for you to go to Park
School," she says. "Do you know when you are due?"

I told her May 4th, and we worked out that I will stay
until the end of this marking period, and then I will transfer to
Park School for Pregnant Girls for the rest of the school year.
I'll be able to come back to Ottawa Hills next year, and it feels
good to have someone looking out for me. Getting a plan and
encouragement is more than I expected when I walked into the
office. I leave feeling like I might be able to handle this. At
least she is the first person who doesn't say my life is over.

The building is on the corner of Fulton and Fuller, The
Booth Salvation Army building. A small part inside of the
building is set aside for the school. I have to take the number
two bus downtown and transfer to the city bus. It's the same
bus I took to high school--south to Ottawa Hills, north to Park
School. When I sit on the bus, I feel embarrassed—being one
of all those pregnant girls getting off the bus that second bus
together. I have heard people talk about those Park School
Girls. If you go and you are pregnant, you are bad. I don't care
because I am happy; I am going to have a baby who is going to
love me. I am going to school, and I am not going to drop out. I
have to make a life for my baby.

I cried last night but today is better. I wonder, *why am I
here?* What I really wish is to be at Ottawa Hills High School. I
want to be with Rennie and get to do all the things we do in
school and after class. I know my life will be different now.
But I have to make sure I do everything right. I'm still scared
that Daddy Mark and Mama Betty will take away my baby and
adopt it for themselves. I must be ready.

I walk in and see more of us girls with protruding
stomachs. Most of the girls are from Grand Rapids and look
like me. We aren't required to go to Park School, but the

counselors encourage us to go because they think we might get hurt in regular school. Velma doesn't go to Park school. The white girls are mostly from far away. They live here at Booth, while the girls from Grand Rapids take the bus like me. This is how rich people take care of their daughters when they get pregnant. Just like there is a hierarchy of foster kids, there is a hierarchy of girls here. One black girl doesn't come all the time, and she is called lazy. Eventually the teacher just forgets about her, but they don't do that to the white girls. Those girls are supposed to go back home and have a life again.

There's more than a color difference between us girls. White girls are looked at like being not-ghetto, so they are treated like they matter, like they will have a future. They either get abortions or end up here and their babies are put up for adoption, so they can continue with school and have the kind of life that white girls are supposed to have. Black girls appeared ghetto, so they are treated like they are lazy and won't amount to anything. When black girls get pregnant, they don't get abortions, maybe because they can't afford them, and they keep their babies, probably because black grandmothers are strong and ready to take care of the whole family. I think that is why others call us ghetto. So, I will try to find a way to be black and non-ghetto. That means I must work hard, harder than anybody else, and prove that I am smart and will take care of my own baby myself.

I meet one white girl from California, and we become friends. She doesn't even have to go outside to get from her bedroom at Booth to school. I sit with her at lunch time because I get teased again for sounding white by some of the other girls. She doesn't want to give up her baby, but her parents are making her. She is a senior in high school, and this is her second baby. Her parents already made her give her first baby to strangers. This makes me feel scared. I didn't know parents could do that, even though I think that Daddy Mark and Mama Betty might take my baby for themselves and send me away since I am adopted. Mama Betty couldn't have kids after Doug--that's why they adopted Shay--and I remember going to see her in the hospital because she had a hysterectomy. Maybe she will want to adopt my baby now, too. I don't like being adopted; I still think of myself as a foster kid because there is no way I feel like Daddy Mark and Mama Betty's kid. I don't want my baby to ever feel like that. My baby will be loved--it will be mine. I have to figure out how to make sure I am the best mother so nobody can take my baby from me.

I am barely showing, but most of the girls have big stomachs. Some people have been there twice. It's a new marking period, but it feels like almost everyone else has been here from the beginning of the school year. The homeroom teacher talks to us and says, "You got to do your work. If you're lazy you're not going to make it here." I take that to heart. Nobody smiles, and they all look me up and down, letting me know they are judging me. I know that soon I will look like them. After a couple of weeks, I started to do math. About a third of the girls didn't know who the father was. About a third were molested by a family member, like me. But not exactly like me because I like Doug. The other girls with older men as fathers strut around like they are important. They get extra clout if the baby daddy picks them up from school. The big thing is that they know their baby's fathers and their baby fathers love them. I feel bad that I can't say anything about Doug. I could have been one of the important girls. There is one girl who is only twelve. She is a tiny, quiet, dark-skinned girl, and she is scared. Everyone says she was raped by a family member, but nobody knows who. I cry for her, feeling so bad.

Mostly, I stay to myself. I do learn a lot from hearing the other girls who look like me who are keeping their babies. The first thing I learned is that you get on welfare and get your own apartment. I wonder if they got pregnant on purpose, especially if it was the second baby. I can see that this gets you out of a bad family home. I don't think I can get welfare or get an apartment because I am adopted. Daddy Mark isn't going to let me get an apartment because he would lose the payments, he gets for me until I am eighteen or graduate high school, which will be even later. Some of the girls know each other, either from their neighborhoods or because they have the same baby father. Those girls get into fights all the time. There is a lot of drama at Park School.

The thing I think about the most is that the girls who know their baby father get to have a family. Will my baby know her father? Will we have a family? Daddy Mark and Mama Betty are still not talking to me, and Doug is pretending it isn't his. I had to tell Rennie why I was leaving school. I didn't tell the other two girls of our four-click team.

Velma isn't getting an apartment. Her parents act like they are happy she is having a baby. They buy her all kinds of beautiful maternity clothes. Her mama throws her a nice baby shower, and she gets all new things for her baby. I am not allowed to have one. It's hard to see Velma get all this attention. Her baby's father stays around for a while. Velma's daddy doesn't like him. But Velma is happy and taken care of, so she drops out of school.

A lot of the girls at Park School won't graduate either, we're told. They mostly drop out after having their kids. I know I won't have any help or any good things for my baby if I don't get them myself. The teachers at Park are different to me—they notice that I talked "proper" and I love my schoolwork or just have read by school files? I am already doing everything I can to take care of and protect my brother and sister. I don't have room to think about someone taking care of me. That sounds like a fairy tale to me and hoping for someone to take care of me will only stop me from doing what I have to do. I don't have any options.

I try to take classes that will help me. I get to have driver's training. The nights when Doug taught me to drive meant I had an easier time than most of the other students. I need to get this done before I get too big because I am worried that I won't be able to drive when I am really big. How would I fit behind the wheel? Will Daddy Mark let me take classes?

I am grateful for my second sewing class, and I learned how to make my own maternity clothes. Daddy Mark won't buy me anything to wear. Miss McConnell teaches me how to sew in Home Economics, and when I tell her I don't have any clothes, she teaches me how to get patterns. I made myself two pairs of pants and two shirts with money I made from Baskin Robbins. One of the tops I sew is a V-neck with a brown flowered fabric, kind of like the dress my daddy sent me when I was eight. These are all the clothes I have to wear throughout my whole pregnancy. Nobody is going to give me any gifts, like Velma's parents gave to her.

I am running out of the money I saved from Baskin Robbins, and I need a job if I am going to take care of my baby. Daddy Mark's best friend's wife is a nurse's aide who works second shift. She needs a babysitter for her two-month-old boy because she has to go back to work. Her schedule changes every week, but she needs me five or six days a week, sometimes on weekends, and a lot of weekdays. Most days after I get done at Park School, I take the bus over to Marnie's and watch her kids, who are six and eight, and newborn. Marnie is white and her husband is black. She seems very frustrated and unhappy with her family, so I wonder if it's like my dad and Vanessa--this is the first bi-racial family I have seen besides them. Or maybe it is the kids. She yells at them a lot. Marnie teaches me how to change diapers, fix a bottle, and rock the baby to sleep. I love taking care of the baby, and even the older kids when they get home from school. I help Leah with her homework and make dinner. It's just like having my own family, and I think of it as on-the-job training. I am getting ready for my baby. I read a lot of parenting books, too.

Sometimes I'm not sure what to do, so I call Marnie at work to ask about heating the bottle and whether it's time to feed the baby. Sometimes William, from ninth grade geometry, comes over. He has a guitar and plays music for us, helping to put the kids to sleep. We talk about our childhoods and our futures. He doesn't try to touch me or do anything, since we are just friends. I love it when he sings to me.

Marnie gets home at 10:30, so she or Henry drives me home. By this time, it's around 11 o'clock, and Daddy Mark and Mama Betty have left me chores to do. I got to do my homework after the kids went to bed, but I'm tired, and I know tomorrow I will have to wake up to take two buses to school, then go to Marnie's, then come home and do chores. My body is heavy and sore, and everything takes a long time. My brain doesn't seem to remember the simplest of tasks; I wash the dishes but don't remember rinsing them. I scrub the floor and it's hard to get up and down, so I don't rinse the rag as often as I should. The drudgery makes me feel exhausted, like life will be one long chore with no relief. I hope that isn't true. I know there is love and happiness. I just have to work hard enough to find it.

I have Sunday off because we aren't allowed to do anything on Sunday, not even play cards. It's a relief to rest a little. I work on Saturdays if Henry and Marnie both have to work, otherwise I get to spend time with Yasmin and Junior.

Rennie isn't allowed to come over now that I'm pregnant. I can go to her house, but I don't have time anymore.

I try to make up for missing Yasmin and Junior the whole week when we are together on Saturday. But there is a Saturday routine. Saturday isn't a day to sleep in and catch up on the rest I need after the rest of the week. We get up early and have a big breakfast. I sit by Yasmin and Junior and food and talk to them. Then we have to do chores. The chores I have to do at 11 at night are nothing compared to Saturday cleaning. This is *'a Daddy-Mark cleaning'*--we wash the walls and scrub everything. I try not to think about how tired I am. I need to be happy for Yasmin and Junior.

As Christmas approaches, I am showing more and more. I have to wear the maternity clothes I sewed every day. By now, it's a standing joke that I never got a doll for Christmas. This makes me sad, so I ask for a doll even though I am way too old for one. It could be a toy for my baby, I think. Each Christmas is less and less like the first, before we got adopted. There aren't very many presents, at least not for Yasmin and Junior and me. But this year there is not a single gift under the tree with a tag that says Regina. I got a paper bag of fruit and candy. Doug gets a lot of gifts, as usual. Nobody punishes him for this.

"Where's my doll?" I ask, trying to make it sound like a joke, so nobody knows how disappointed I am.

"You have your doll in your stomach," Daddy Mark says. And he laughs' his mean laugh. Of the few Christmases I have had; this is the most hurtful. Not celebrating at all was easier than being hurt like this. I struggle to hold back the tears in front of everybody because I don't want to ruin the holiday for Yasmin and Junior. His words feel like a stab wound to my heart and my chest feels like it is exploding in on itself.

Yasmin and Junior and I have our own thing in my bedroom where I give them a little of the money I have earned from babysitting. I'm not allowed to go shopping, and I don't have very much--I'm saving everything for the baby. Even though Marnie has given me some of Joseph's baby clothes as he grows out of them, I know I'll have to pay for everything myself once the baby is born. I *want* to buy everything, so they can't say they are taking care of it. I'm still afraid that Daddy

Mark and Mama Betty will try to take my baby, and I am not going to give them any reason.

I hope I have a boy, so the clothes I have from Marnie will be good, and maybe a boy will make Doug happy. Plus, if my boy is the oldest, he will be able to protect his little sister if he ever has one. We don't know for sure what we are having, but Velma thinks she is going to have a girl, she says, and I am going to have a boy. We think about what we will name our babies, but we can't know if it will be a boy or girl. Until the baby is born, I think of the baby as *it.* I can't wait until my baby has a name, until then I can call it "it". Velma and I love to talk about our babies and what they will be like. Of course, Velma's life is different. Her daddy loves her dearly, and her brothers do everything for her.

After Christmas, I have my sixteenth birthday. Rennie is going to turn sixteen, too, and she says this is a special birthday. Her party is after my birthday, but I don't go because I think she would be embarrassed to have her best friend pregnant at her party. She doesn't say this, but Rennie's mother knows what happened and isn't happy. Daddy Mark and Mama Betty have told me to stop telling Rennie so much again because she tells her mom everything. Nobody celebrates my birthday. "You don't get anything. You're sixteen and you have a baby in your stomach," Daddy Mark says to me. We usually don't get anything for birthdays anyway, but I hoped that sixteen would be different because in our culture it's special. There is no sweet sixteen for me, but I think that at least I will be sixteen when I have my baby, not fifteen. Somehow that seems better.

For the first time, I am disappointed with myself. I have been too busy and overwhelmed to stop and think about my life. Mostly I have been focusing on my baby and trying to make sure it has everything I didn't have. I am so careful to do everything right. Even though I'm not allowed to go out and go shopping, I am allowed to go to the grocery store with Daddy Mark. He buys groceries every week at Big Top. I sneak and buy treats for Yasmin and Junior. I also bought *Parents* magazine. It tells mothers what to eat and to be active, so labor won't be as hard. I keep track of all the food I eat and exercise every day. I am learning about how to be a mother. My baby will have a mama who sticks around, who loves and cares, and who won't let anybody else take it or hurt it. But now, I wonder what I look like to everybody else.

The thing I miss the most is going to Rennie's house after school. It's the place where all the popular kids go to hang out. Her mom keeps the refrigerator stocked, and anybody can just go in and take what they want to eat. I am amazed that this is possible. I don't remember ever living in a place where I could take food if I wanted. The kids danced and drank and smoked cigarettes. I tried smoking, but those things are nasty, but for a while I felt like I was part of something, a group of friends, even if they were mostly Rennie's friends. Everybody treated me like I belonged. Now I am at work when they are all having fun. I wonder if they miss me.

Chapter 18

Birth and Rebirth

"There is a wonderous curiosity in every young mother. It is a strange miracle to see, to hold a living being formed in and coming out of one's self." —Simone De Beauvoir

I know I am really pregnant now; my belly is getting big. Doug stops paying attention to me, but I don't care because I am getting ready for my baby. When Marnie has a weekday off, I come home from school and sit on the bottom of the stairs to do my homework. I like to sit in the foyer with the door open to feel the warm April air. The kids play outside while I study. Mama Betty is still at work, and Daddy Mark is always gone someplace. It's a nice and quiet place to study every day. Until one day, Doug comes home while I am sitting there, eight months pregnant, and barely able to move. He tells me to get up and go to the top of the stairs. I've been ignoring him, but for some reason, I feel I must listen to what he tells me. I get to the top of the stairs, and he makes me bend over. He struggles to take down my pants and I wait. He has sex with me from behind, saying bent over the steps is the only way he can get to me. I wait until he is done and go back to my homework. Did this hurt the baby? I asked. He says, I don't know. But he wouldn't have done it if it would, I think. It didn't hurt but I felt pressure down there.

A couple of weeks later, I am sitting on the landing again after dinner, and I pee my pants. I go upstairs and change. Then I pee again, and I think something isn't right. It's like the books I have been reading about pregnancy and labor. I think my water broke, so I called out to Daddy Mark and Mama Betty. Mama Betty says she headed out shopping with her sister. I call the doctor, and I'm told to I have to go to the hospital. Daddy Mark gets the car. He tells Doug to stay home. Yasmin and Junior watch while I waddle out to the car, but they can't come either. It's just me and Daddy Mark going to the hospital. Daddy Mark is still mad at me, so he doesn't talk to me during the whole drive to the hospital.

He takes me into the hospital, and I am admitted to my room. I can hear the nurse outside say, "Oh my god, she's only sixteen." I stay in the room all by myself until the nurse and doctor come in. While I am waiting, I remember what I had for dinner, a pork chop sandwich. I think my baby is going to have a pork chop birthmark. Everybody says babies are born with a birthmark that is something that happened to the mama. I think my baby will probably also hate ice cream. At Park School, they taught us everything about labor, so I know how to breathe. I think how lucky I am to have my teachers--nobody else ever told me anything. The pain starts. They are five minutes apart as I look at the big clock on the wall. No one is with me as I go through the labor. Nobody to hold my hand, to say breath Regina with each contraction. After about six hours since I peed my pants, I am headed to the delivery room. Lots of light, a doctor and multiple nurses. Never been in a room like this. Whoa, the pain is getting really bad. They say after checking my pelvis I am dilated to nine. I remember the books and school. That means its time. And no turning back. I am about to become a mother. A teenage mother. A teenager that will be loved no matter what. It is all worth it because I'll have my baby.

The nurse put my legs up in the stirrups and a doctor sat in between them. The pain was the worst, except when they told me to push. Pushing seemed to help. Mentally it felt good knowing I was having my first child. Before I knew it the doctor said, "it's a girl". I cried when they put her on my chest while they did other things down there. The nurse says to me, you did really well.

Later, I hear the nurses talking outside the room, saying, "She did well. Most young girls scream and call for their mama." I was quiet, concentrating on what I had to do. Pain is normal for me; I never thought about screaming and I don't have a mama to call out for.

In a way I feel like I am an outsider watching myself, curious to see if this is the way *Parents* said it would be. The labor was less than seven hours from the time my water broke to her birth. "Hello, beautiful, I love you," I say when they put her in my arms. Before I knew it, they took my baby away to weigh her and check her. They told us about this at Park School, too. The nurse asked me what to name her. I have known since I was twelve when I decided if I had a daughter, I would name her Tia. Her middle name is after Doug's favorite basketball player, Mychal Thompson. I spell it for a girl, Mychelle. Then they took her to the nursery across from the door to my room.

Daddy Mark must have left the hospital and come back with Mama Betty. Why didn't he bring Doug? I wonder if it's because Daddy Mark is still mad at me. I can hear Daddy Mark in the hallway talking to Betty. He says, "Betty, this is Doug's baby because she looks just like you." I gasped because I didn't know they still thought it wasn't Doug's. How is that possible? What has Doug been telling them?

When everybody leaves, I walk to the nursery. It hurts to take each step, and I feel like everyone is looking at me as I step into the hallway. I see Tia and am amazed at her. She has black curly hair and it's long, longer than I think a baby would have. I guess the old wives' tale is true, heartburn meant the baby's hair was growing. I'm disappointed to see that she does look like Betty. I wanted her to look like me, to be mine only. She did have the one trait I hoped she wouldn't get. That is my upper lip without a crease. Suddenly I am scared. We have lied and kept the secret that Doug is my baby's father, but everybody will know now. The lie is out. I worry again that they might take her away from me, but I can't let that happen.

In the nursery, I sit on the rocking chair and concentrate on my baby. She is beautiful and wonderful. I look at her tiny fingers and toes. I look into that little face, and I say, "I'm going to raise you the way I wish I had been raised. I'm going to love you no matter what, and I'm going to teach you to say, 'I love you.'" Just like I taught Yasmin and Junior to say, "I love you." I kissed and hugged them all the time, so they know I love them. I am happy that my real family, my blood family, is getting bigger.

I think about my dad. He doesn't know that I have a baby because I haven't been able to see him, and even when I have written him letters, I haven't told him. I know that soon I will be old enough, though, and he will be able to meet Tia. The surprising thing is that I miss *her*. And when I realize how much I love Tia, I start to wonder why *she* didn't love me this much. It is clearer than ever that something was wrong with me, that I didn't deserve love.

I am staying in the hospital for the standard three days. Everyone comes to see Tia and me, and that makes me happy. Some aunts come, but nobody says anything about Tia being Doug's baby. All of my friends from school come, from Ottawa Hills, and I feel special and popular. I haven't seen a lot of them since I had to go to Park School, so I am surprised they even remember me. The only other time I was in the hospital was when Frankie Mae took us to get away from Aunt Karen finding us, and that time was scary. This time is not so bad. I have Tia with me when she isn't in the nursery. Doug never comes to the hospital, but he will get to see Tia when we get home.

When it comes time to take my baby home, I hope it is a clear day. I don't want her to see snow until next year, when she will be almost one, and we can go outside and play while the snowflakes sprinkle us with magic. I'm a little sad on April 28th when we step out of the hospital doors to get in Daddy Mark's car, and it is snowing.

I am totally responsible for taking care of Tia. Doug doesn't help, and Daddy Mark doesn't seem interested. I still have my *Parents* magazine, which tells me everything to do, and what is best for the baby. I have to get cloth diapers because I can't afford Pampers. Mama Betty offers to buy Pampers, but I tell her no. I'm still afraid that they will say they are paying for the baby, so they can take her away. I won't let that happen.

When it comes time to change Tia and I have a few poopy diapers, I ask Mama Betty about how to wash them. She gives me a bucket full of water and tells me to go downstairs and wash the diapers myself. *Parents* magazine says a new mother shouldn't carry heavy weights or walk up and down stairs too much, but I don't have a choice. I lug the bucket downstairs, stepping as carefully as possible to avoid the pain, and wash my baby's diapers by myself. I had already washed the clothes and blankets Marnie gave me and had everything ready. Marnie sold me a crib, too. Having everything ready made it easier. I hope I can get some girl clothes for Tia soon, so she doesn't look like a boy.

Parents also recommend breastfeeding. I want to do everything right for Tia, so I will try it. Everybody laughs at me and tells me I'm crazy. At Park School, they had us apply for WIC. While I was pregnant, they gave me the extra milk I needed to make sure my baby was strong. Now I can get coupons for formula, and I use them instead of breastfeeding. I still get to hold her and cuddle and love her. Junior and Yasmin are so happy. Yasmin holds her all the time, pretending Tia is her little sister. Junior likes to let Tia grab his fingers. They hover around her, and I'm glad I have taught them to be loving and kind.

My friend Teresa asked me to bring Tia over to show her mother. I am so proud of my baby. I dress her up in the best clothes we have, something that is cute and not too boyish. She has a big afro, even as a baby, and I make sure it looks pretty. My baby is beautiful. Everyone who sees Tia loves her. And compliments her thick curly hair. When I get to Teresa's house, she lets me in, and I go to see her mama. I don't really know her, but I think it's nice that she wants to see Tia.

"She looks normal," Teresa's mother says. I'm confused. Why would my perfect, beautiful baby be anything but normal? I asked her what she meant. "When you have a baby with your brother, that baby won't be right."

"He's not my real brother. I'm adopted." Even though I know everyone thinks of Doug as my brother, I never really thought of him as a brother--either because at first, he was so mean to me and I didn't like him, or because when I got older, he treated me like a friend. I never thought of Shay as my sister, either. Even if she was little, she was spoiled, and she was the reason Yasmin and Junior got beat all the time. I had been angry when I first got there and didn't want a family. It took me until Doug was nice to me to even feel like we had any connection at all. Of all the times Mama Betty said that blood was thicker than water, this time was the one that I was most relieved about since she will treat my baby right.

"That's why everyone from school went to the hospital," Teresa says. "Rennie told us you were pregnant by your brother." I don't understand this. I am startled when I hear this, followed by hurt and feeling of betrayal. Rennie knows I'm adopted. Her parents knew Mama Betty and Daddy Mark before we even got here. Why would she say that? Teresa was always jealous of my friendship with Rennie. Maybe this was her way of breaking us up. But I'm too scared of losing

Rennie's friendship to do anything. I will never ask Rennie why she said it.

Rennie's mom says Tia needs to be blessed, and she wants to be Tia's godmother. I call her Ma Doris because she is the closest person I have to a mom. The godfather is Mama Betty's favorite sister's husband, Alex, who used to come to the CB Club and hang around me all the time. He asked to be Tia's godfather. We all go to Ma Doris's church for the monthly blessing of the babies. Mama Betty and Daddy Mark won't have us go to their church. I know Daddy Mark would get mad if we put it out there that I had a baby with Doug. I go to Rennie's house a lot with Tia, and Ma Doris loves her.

Ryder and I broke up when I got pregnant, but he is still friends with Doug. He comes over, and even though I like him, I know he won't be my boyfriend again. When he comes over and sees Tia, he says he knows the baby is Doug's. He tells me he isn't mad. "If I was Doug, I would have done the same thing." That's his response.

My feelings are all confused. I don't feel bad that I did what Doug wanted me to do because I didn't have any choice, but I feel bad about lying to Ryder. I can tell Ryder is hurt because he doesn't talk to me for a while after we break up-- even though he keeps talking to Doug. For some reason, he doesn't get mad at Doug. It's like everyone thinks it's my fault. There must be something wrong with me, maybe something wrong with all girls, especially the ones who want so badly to be loved. Now, I don't have Ryder, and I don't want Doug. Even if Doug says he is a player, though he says I am his main squeeze. I'm mad that Doug doesn't take care of Tia financially, so I'm not sure it's such a good thing to be his main squeeze.

Most of the time, Daddy Mark won't let me take Tia any place, just to visit cousins. Then I'm finally allowed to bring Tia to Rennie's house and even go to her family functions again. This is such a relief that I forget about what Teresa said Rennie told everyone. It turns out that I don't have time to hang out much anymore, though. I have a baby to take care of, but then I must get a job, too. When I go downstairs, Daddy Mark is at the dining room table, and there is a bill on it. I am holding Tia, so I have to adjust her so I can see what Daddy Mark is trying to show me. It is the bill from the hospital to pay for Tia's birth. "You're gonna have to pay for that," he says. It's more than $200, and I don't know how I'm going to do it. Doug has his job, working part-time at Sears, and he makes some money, but nobody asks him to pay for the birth of his baby, and he doesn't offer. He likes nice clothes and albums, and that is what he spends his money on. He doesn't do anything to take care of Tia or buy her clothes or anything.

I have to get a job. Knowing that my daughter has only me to rely on makes me feel strong and determined. I am an adult now, totally responsible for another human being. I have to protect her, and I have to make a plan to get us both out of here, so we will be safe.

Rennie and I went to a neighborhood hospital. They are hiring kids to bring meal trays to the rooms. Rennie got the job, but they tell me I can't work until my baby is six weeks old. My heart sinks and I feel so tired and defeated. How am I supposed to pay for the hospital bill and take care of Tia? I go to another place, an insurance company, and I don't tell them about Tia. I have learned that keeping secrets is the only way to get what I want. They have me take some tests and then call me. They say they are impressed with how great I did on my tests. I am going to be a full-time file clerk this summer. Each week I hand Daddy Mark some money to pay off my hospital bill, knowing that it will take me even longer to save. Mama Betty is happy because her pastor's daughter is working there too. I don't tell them that I lied on the application about my age or about having to go back to school. I need this job, and I do good work. Maybe I will go to night school. However, Daddy Mark tells me that I have to go back to school, Ottawa Hills High. Remembering how my counselor had told me I could come back next school year, I am excited and determined to go back. With only two weeks of work left, I've paid off the hospital bill for Tia; I was too scared of Daddy Mark not to. I'm worried that when I go back to school, I won't be able to afford all the things I need for Tia. But I will have to find a way.

I am going to graduate, so I have to quit my job to go back to school. I take five classes in eleventh grade. Then for two hours during lunch, I tutored at Shay's school for two more credits. I am a teacher's aide for the fourth grade. Every day I look forward to reading to the students or teaching them how to do their math problems. This doesn't feel like a job at all— more like playing. It's just like teaching Yasmin and Junior when we played school. I can't wait until I can teach these things to Tia, too. Now, I know I really want to be a teacher and doing this will help me. After school and on weekends, I babysit for Marnie sometimes when I can, but I still don't make enough money. Marnie helps me apply for a job at the nursing home where she works. If I get this job, I can go to school, tutor at Shay's school, then work at the nursing home second shift. All this for my baby. For Tia.

In *Spectator* class, when I return to OHHS, Mr. Stanley asks me to write about what it is like to be a teenage mother. Even though in journalism class we are supposed to write newspaper articles, Mr. Stanley thinks my personal essay will help a lot of kids understand how hard it is to be a teen mother, and maybe it will make them think first. The first time I wrote about it and showed him my article, he said I am too graphic, so I have to rewrite. The headline of the article is "Living with It" and I write everything about having Tia. I still can't put in that Doug is the father, not in school, but I write about being pregnant, having a baby, and going to school.

Living With It

I felt scared and alone. I had just recieved some shocking news. I was eight weeks pregnant. Of course I cried, but it was no use. Crying wouldn't make me not pregnant. So I said to myself, "You're just going to have to accept the fact that you are pregnant."

Telling my parents was the hardest thing to do. I didn't want to disappoint them. But I had no choice. My mother didn't believe me but my father took it hard. He convinced my mother that I was pregnant. There was an unusual quietness around the house that day.

My baby's father didn't act the way I thought he would. He was angry. He figured his life and mine were ruined. It was hard to take. He wanted me to have an abortion. He felt that I was too young to take care of a child and I'd be tied down for the rest of my life. He didn't want to marry me, although I wouldn't have married him on the basis of a child. Yes, I loved him at the time but he didn't share the same feeling with me. That didn't help the burden of the pregnancy.

When I was about 12 weeks along, I started prenatal care because I decided I was going to have a nice, healthy baby alone. The father, at the time, began adjusting to the fact that he was going to be a father regardless of what he wanted.

I also changed schools. I started Park in the beginning of the 2nd marking period. I was a sophomore.

My life began to get back to normal in some ways. The daily routine was school, home, babysitting, and housework, then homework. That went on

was to be born.

I began to get really excited. I felt as though I was adjusting all over again to the fact that I was going to be a mother. I think the father was getting excited too, although he tried not to show it.

In the third week of April I stay home from school. The day I started the procedures to do, the birth of my baby awaited me that evening.

I started having labor pains and my water bag leaked. I hoped I was going to have my baby.

At the hospital the doctor took a test on me to see if I was in labor. I passed. He said within twenty four hours I was going to have my baby. I was more excited than I'd ever been before. To my surprise I was scared. I just wanted to get through it okay.

Labor lasted 4½ hours from the 1st pain. At 1:47 AM April 25, I had a very healthy 8 lb., 4½ oz. girl. She was 20½ long. They laid her on my chest and I said, "She is really mine. I had her."

I really didn't accept the fact that she was my baby and I loved her more than anything in the world.

Her father began to love her. He was proud of his daughter. He saw her and me every day and helped me take care of her.

Now my daughter is nine months old and still healthy and very active.

Her father is very attached to her and so am I. I don't regret having my baby, but my desire to be with her keeps me from going out so much. Most of the time I don't mind.

Being pregnant and having a baby is harder than I pictured it to be. But I'm doing okay, now.

Doug and Mama Betty are taking care of Tia every day now, and I don't get to see her enough. One statistic they told us in Park School was, that if you get pregnant before you are eighteen, you will most likely have a second child before eighteen. Because of this, I don't let Doug touch me all summer, not just because his parents finally believe Tia is his, but because they are doing more for her than he is, buying diapers, playing with her, loving her. Doug still does not contribute one dime to her care. I always thought the father was supposed to work and pay—like the pastor at our church always said. I still had to pay the hospital bill. But Doug tries to have sex with me again. It has been a long time--Tia is four months old. He makes me lie down on the couch, just like he used to. It seems like this is going to start again, so I tell him that I have to go on the Pill. I evade him after that one time. I went to Planned Parenthood to get on the Pill a couple of weeks later because I know that I can't say no. He is my baby's daddy, and I know I have to do what he wants to have any hope of having some kind of family with him. I will do what I have to do to make sure Tia grows up with her father and her mother.

Just when I thought I was settling into a routine I noticed after my visit to Planned Parenthood to get on the pill, my period hadn't started. I told Doug about this. He said go back to the clinic. So, I did. They did a pregnancy test. It was positive. Doug was waiting outside in the car. He didn't make me take the bus. I told him and he got really mad. He said you must have an abortion. I agree because I immediately think with two babies his parents will definitely take Tia, and I won't finish school. I am so scared. Abortion is murder and God won't forgive me. But won't he understand?

I scheduled the abortion and told Doug he has to take me and pick me up. He stresses that I must not tell anyone, even my best friends, Rennie and Taylor. Before I know it, I'm at my fourth appointment at Planned Parenthood. But this one is way different. The nurse explained what was going to happen and gave me pamphlets about how to take care of myself afterwards.

I'm on a table in the same physical position I was in when Tia came into the world. But now, I feel this sucking sensation as I hear the motor humming. It only took a few minutes. Wow, a few minutes to take a life but several to bring one into the world. Will God forgive me. I know I couldn't have this baby. Daddy Mark would probably beat it out of me anyway. Beat me worse than when I was unknowingly two months pregnant with Tia. I must forget this happened and take those pills every day. Because I know Doug will still want to have sex. Nothing stops him.

I remind myself that I have to save money to take care of Tia, and I have to save enough so we can move out as soon as I graduate from high school. Weekends are good, though. I take Tia to Park School, and they have classes about how to be a good mother. I want to make sure that I do everything right with her--and now I also must make up for the time I am away, the time she is with Mama Betty and Doug instead of me. Tia is smart and strong. At five months she stands and walks by holding onto furniture. She seems to unite the whole family. It doesn't feel like it's their family against us three kids anymore. Daddy Mark and Mama Betty play with her while I am at school and work. They don't really tell me about what her day is like, but the little bit of time I get to spend with her, I see how wonderful she is. Every time I leave her with them, I have to fight back the terror that they will find a way to adopt her and take her away from me. When I come home and see her sleeping in her crib, I feel relief and joy. I pray hard all the time for me to be able to keep my baby.

Juniors Elected to the National Honor Society

Bancroft, Anne	Curie, Ellen	Greskowiak, Susan	Novitsk
Bander, Stephanie	Czetli, Shane	*Helder, Thomas	*Ott, W
Bateson, Amy	Datema, Douglas	Hendrickson, Anne	Pecemy
Beckering, Martha	David, Charese	Hendrickson, John	Reed, S
Beemer, Greg	Davis, Revester	Heydenburg, Lisa	Roberts
*Berman, Ruth	DeBruyne, Beth	Hoffman, Cindy	Robinsc
*Beukema, Steve	DeVinney, Sharon	Holst, Wanda	Robinsc
Bickel, Wayne	Dimitriou, Jim	Hough, Stephanie	Sayhe,
Binder, James	Doyle, Richard	Jackson, Linda	Shipp,
Block, Sheryl	Duiven, David	*Johnson, Gigi	Sisson,
*Blouw, Jaci	Eaddy, Michelle	Jones, Roberta	Smith,
Boylen, Chris	Erickson, Brenda	Karp, Pamela	TenHav
Bradley, Brenda	Ferguson, Maureen	Lambert, Kelly	The, Jef
*Bridges, Patti	Ferrante, Sandra	Mangus, Bryan	Thomps
*Browneye, Kristin	Fetz, Cheryl	*Manwaring, Mary	Vanderl
*Budde, Jane	*Flanagan, Beth	*Mattaliano, Diane	Williams
Burns, Donald	Garceau, James	*McLiechey, Gina	Winberg
Carowitz, Michael	Gietsen, Janet	Metzger, Kathy	Whmer,
Chalker, Harry	Goeldel, Joseph	Mohan, Mary	Zadvins!
Collins, Regina	Grant, Amy	*Nelson, Donna	Zervos,

*Denotes New Member

139

I start eleventh grade, and I am inducted into the National Honor Society, one of the few black students. Daddy Mark and Mama Betty don't seem to care, even though Daddy Mark keeps telling me I must get the best grades. They got a letter, but don't bother to take me to the ceremony. Even so, I have overheard Daddy Mark bragging about my grades. He never says anything to me, though, except to warn me that I'll get in trouble if I don't get all As. It's up to me to decide about school, and I try to pick classes that will help me. I am on the newspaper staff. Which is how I learned about the Induction to the Honor Society. I had to go get pictures of the students from the school photographer. I felt a twinge seeing the few black students' pictures and I wasn't a part of. Some were my friends. So, they asked me why wasn't I there? I said I didn't know about it. Nonetheless, I had to write the story of who got inducted and how you are elected.

Top Students Join National Honor Society

by Regina Collins

The National Honor Society is a national organization of sophomores, juniors, and seniors who have a GPA of 3.00 or more. They must also be recommended by teachers. The purpose of the National Honor Society is to provide service to the school.

To be eligible for membership students must be a Junior or Senior according to Ottawa's guidelines. The next step is to let Mrs. Montgomery know you are interested. She then checks your GPA and sends it around to all the teachers. From there the teachers' vote on the students in leadership, character, and service to the school. So just having a higher than 3 point average doesn't automatically make students members. They must be judged and voted on by the teachers.

The officers have been elected. They are: President Joe Shoemaker, Vice-President Randy Rosema, Treasurer Kris Koetsier and Secretary Phyllis O'Conner.

If you have any questions concerning National Honor Society see Mrs. Montgomery in the North House on the third floor.

On school days, I wake up around 5:30 to spend time with Tia. I get her dressed and feed her before I leave. I go to school early for an extra class, take a number two bus home and then walk to Shay's school to tutor. It's only two blocks back so I walk home for lunch and to see Tia before I have to be at work at 2:30. I work until 10:30 at night and then come home to do homework and the chores Daddy Mark left for me. Sometimes, if I'm lucky I can do homework on my breaks at work, then I can get to bed hopefully by midnight.

In the middle of eleventh grade, just before semester break and right after by 17th birthday. I have a meeting with my counselor again to discuss my schedule. I tell her I need to hurry through school, maybe do night school too so I can take care of Tia. She says that I have enough credits to graduate this year and that with my grades, I can qualify for a scholarship to college. A whole year early? I am so excited and happy as I walk out of the office with the letter to give to Daddy Mark for graduation. I haven't told anyone of my plan to move out. I will be seventeen when I graduate, so Daddy Mark and Mama Betty will still get the money from the state of Michigan until I am supposed to graduate at eighteen. Daddy Mark might not sign to let me graduate early, but I don't let that stop me. I pray about it, that Daddy Mark won't be like Grandmo, who wouldn't let me move ahead a grade because of my cousins. Surprisingly Daddy Mark signs, probably thinking it would be embarrassing for him if I ended up dropping out. Just like that I am now a senior in high school. Graduating in just five months.

Soon after, Yasmin comes to me, scared to talk. She tells me that she is pregnant. The daddy is another boy she hangs around with at Franklin Park. He's just thirteen, like her. She is scared, and we don't know what to do. I tell her for now that she has to hide it until we figure out what to do. I am upset because me and Rennie had told her about getting pregnant. We told her we would take her to the clinic to go on the Pill. She told us that she wasn't having sex. I have been so busy that I didn't notice anything about her change. I want to shout, "No, no, no," but instead I try to think about how I can protect Yasmin, what I can do. I know for sure that as soon as I graduate, I have to move out. I have to take Yasmin and Junior and Tia someplace safe.

Chapter 19

College Dreams

"A winner is a dreamer who never gives up." — Nelson Mandela

Because I am graduating early, Mrs. Brown, my counselor, helps me apply for a scholarship. I am awarded a full ride to Grand Valley State University—in accounting, one of two recipients selected. Once they find out I am a teenage mother, they revoke my scholarship because they say I'd most likely fail anyway. I am devastated. How am I going to take care of my baby? I can't just keep working at the nursing home. I am also accepted at Eastern Michigan University, where Mrs. Brown had me apply because they have on-campus childcare and housing. Doug says I can't go. It looks like I won't be able to go to college.

So many of the people I know or grew up around seem to be just in survival mode. They're happy if they can make enough to get by and pay the bills. Their lives are so focused on just having enough food and a place to live that they can't even think about more, about going to college, pursuing success, reaching down and carrying their families and others out of poverty. For some reason, I had always wanted more than that, for myself, for my sister and brother, for my children. It was so difficult for me to face that I might be one of them, just working at a low-paying job and buying cheap food and paying rent. The thought brought tears to my eyes, but I pushed them back, pushed back my doubts, and told myself that I would find a way. Maybe not now, but some day, someday soon.

Even if I can't go to college, I know I can't stay at Daddy Mark and Mama Betty's. If I get out of there, then I can make sure they don't take my baby. They love her like they never loved any of us, who they didn't get to have from birth— except Doug, who was the prized child for the whole family— and Shay, they spoil her. I know they think of her as only *their* blood. I started thinking of a plan to move out as soon as I graduate. I buy necessary things for Tia, like a highchair, but I save up as much money as I can, so I will be able to move.

Christmas with Tia is going to be better than any Christmas I have ever had. I am working, so I have some money. I can buy real gifts for Tia, Yasmin, and Junior. Tia turns 8 months on Christmas. I am excited because there is a two-week break, and I will have time to spend with Tia. She has started walking, but I haven't seen her do it yet. For a special treat, I got her ears pierced. This way people will know she is not a boy, even in her hand-me-down boy clothes. Mama Betty and Daddy Mark get a lot of gifts for Tia --they know she is theirs. They buy her clothes and toys. Girl's clothes, which is good. It feels like we are all almost a real family. I don't even care that I only get a bag of fruit and candy again. I have the best doll ever now that I have Tia. Even Doug gets her gifts. Shay and Doug, as always, got a lot from Mama Betty and Daddy Mark, but this year, I can make it up to Yasmin and Junior by getting them some gifts too. I feel happy.

For my seventeenth birthday, I decided I want to celebrate. This is the first time I will ever have a birthday party. Daddy Mark, and Doug are at work. Since I earn my own money, I buy a birthday cake. My first birthday cake. There is a bakery near us, and I figured out how to order a cake from them myself. I want chocolate cake with bright colored icing, I have them write "Happy Birthday Regina!" on it in white. It's decorated with balloons, too. I'm so happy when I go to pick it up. We can't have it until after dinner, but once Mama Betty leaves us to do the dishes, I pull out the cake. We clear the table, and Yasmin lights the candles. They sing "Happy Birthday" to me while Tia won't sit in her highchair, she's stands beside me. I am seventeen and she is almost nine months now. When I blow out the candles, I make a wish that I will be able to make a better life for us all. My friends celebrated their birthdays multiple times, with lots of family and with friends, our age. I should miss that, but I am happy to at least have this celebration with my real family.

Yasmin is starting to show, and we can't hide it anymore. We have to tell Daddy Mark, and I say I will do it for her. She is laying down in bed when Daddy Mark gets home. I go down to tell him just like I did when it was me. He isn't expecting any bad news, and nobody has paid attention to the fact that Yasmin is getting bigger. She is still growing, anyway. When I tell Daddy Mark, he doesn't storm out like he did when I told him I was pregnant. Instead, he rushes up to Yasmin and starts beating her in her bed. He says he is going to beat the baby out of her, just like his daddy tried with his sister. I am shocked and scared, and I cry and scream, but I can't make him stop. He beats her, and she just lays there, huddled in a pile of blankets. When he finally stops, it's like all the air has rushed out of the room, out of my lungs. The whole world stops, and there is just Yasmin, huddled on the bed crying. Daddy Mark leaves without saying anything else, and I try to take care of Yasmin. She cries and I feel so bad for her. Yasmin is in so much pain that she has to miss school for two days, but it didn't work. Daddy Mark didn't make her lose her baby.

I'm graduating with a 3.8 GPA out of 4.0. *As an adult I learned my GPA held the record for the highest GPA of any minority graduate for ten years until Mrs. Brown daughter broke it.* –It even included the honors classes I'd taken. Mrs. Brown helped me to understand what college is and how important it is, so I tell myself that even if I can't go right away, I will find my chance.

The day before my graduation ceremony, I felt nervous and happy. I feel like a grownup. I am graduating a year ahead of my class, so I only know a few of the kids I am graduating with--the ones who were in my honors classes. There are no parties for me to go to, and the best I get is having a drink with Rennie in her car. There's a store that sells to minors, so Rennie goes in and gets a bottle of Southern Comfort for us to share. I don't get to go to my Prom--that will be next year when I am gone. Daddy Mark and Mama Betty don't have a special dinner or anything. I have Tia, Yasmin, and Junior to hug me and make me feel proud.

I have paid for my cap and gown and honors cords. I paid for my senior pictures—Daddy Mark will no longer pay for my school pictures, even though this the last one. You'd think he'd be proud. It's ok because I want to make this day feel special. I was happy to buy the dress I'd wear under my graduation gown. Babysitting monies really helped.

I have never cut my hair before; nobody has ever thought to take me to a beauty salon. Velma and Rennie go to beauty salons. I made an appointment, thinking Daddy Mark might be mad, but now that I am an adult, I can do what I want to my own hair. The salon is small and cramped at the end of the block. The hairdresser is a black lady, too. She starts cutting and styling my hair. I can see the piles of my long afro falling to the floor around me in puddles. I had a lot of hair. Now my hair is short and pressed flat to my head with little curls. I'm not sure I like it--I don't look like me. I don't care, this is my decision, and I can do what I want. When I get home, Daddy Mark goes off about my hair. I don't like making him mad, and my feelings are hurt, but there is nothing I can do now. When I put on my graduation cap, only a few little curls showed. That is my statement of independence.

At graduation, in June, I wore my National Honor Society cords as I walked to get my diploma. Daddy Mark and Mama Betty bring Yasmin and Junior and Shay to the ceremony. Doug stays home with Tia. Now I know I am free, I am grown up, I am about to start my own life.

First Born Middle Child

After graduation, life gets a little easier. I just have to work full-time, no school or tutoring, so I can be with Tia more. I have saved up enough to move out, just like I promised myself. I took bookkeeping in high school, so I know how to make a budget. With my full-time job at the nursing home, I should be able to pay rent and buy most anything we need. Doug takes me apartment hunting and we find a place in Burton Heights that has two bedrooms for $200 a month, including utilities. I don't tell anybody what I'm planning to do, except Yasmin and Junior. I feel horrible about leaving them, but I have to protect Tia. I tell them that they will be able to come and see me and stay overnight sometimes. Maybe my apartment will be the safe place they come to when they need to. I try not to cry, and so do they. I keep saying over and over that they can come and see me any time.

My lease starts on July 1, but I must wait until it's safe. I have been folding and packing clothes so they will be ready to go when I am. I take apart Tia's crib and have her sleep with me, so I won't have to take extra time when I leave. Nobody goes into my room, so it's okay. On July 3, when Daddy Mark goes to the store to buy food for the holiday weekend, I think right away that this is my chance. He's the only one who will stop me, so I have to go while he is gone. Mama Betty is home, but she doesn't try to stop me. The only thing she says is, "You know your daddy's going to be mad." I know, but I don't care. Once I'm gone, they can't control me. Nothing is going to stop me. Doug helps me pack up the station wagon and drives me to the new apartment. I take my twin bed, which Doug ties on top of the station wagon, and Tia's crib and highchair, and our clothes and a few little items that will fit in the car. That's all we have for the first week. Doug rushes to help me get everything into the apartment, but I have to put it all together and unpack because he has to get back before Daddy Mark comes home. I learn to put together the bed and crib on my own. When I'm done, I'm so tired that Tia and I sleep together in my bed all night.

On July 4, I woke up in my own apartment. While everyone else is having parties with family and friends to celebrate Independence Day, I am alone with Tia celebrating my own independence. There is no way to describe the feeling of freedom and hope I am experiencing. I have done it, just like I said; I am on my own and in control of my own life.

The next weekend, I go to the Salvation Army to buy all my kitchen stuff. I got a table and two chairs and a green couch with a hideaway bed. I used some of the money I saved up. The Salvation Army is close enough to walk, but Doug actually comes and helps me drive over there and get the stuff back to my apartment. I love doing all the things that make me a grownup with my own home.

When I found my apartment, I didn't know very much about Burton Heights. It is a scary place. And it's lonely. My friends, like Rennie and Taylor, think it's cool that I am a grownup with my own place, but they aren't able to come over very often. Yasmin and Junior are far away--it would take a bus ride to get here, so I only see them when I go to them. Doug isn't allowed to visit, but he comes to pick up Tia when I have to go to work. One thing I have is going to Park School for parenting classes. They have a ride program, and a car comes to pick me up. I live on the second floor, so it takes me a while to get down to where the car is waiting. One night it takes too long. When I got there, the driver is pulling away. I try to chase him with Tia in my arms, but he doesn't look back. I know I have to get better at planning. I cry. I cried really hard. I am lonely.

Church is my one bright spot during my lonely, scary weeks in Burton Heights. Daddy Mark actually lets Doug pick up me and Tia and take us to their church. They have started going to a new church called Messiah Missionary Baptist Church, and I like the pastor, plus I get to see Yasmin and Junior. I feel a little embarrassed because I am a teenage mom and out of wedlock. Doug doesn't seem to care, and he usually doesn't stay for church anyway. He has his own car to pick us up and drop us off. The pastor talks about being evenly yoked. That means that the husband and wife are tied together, just like a pair of horses leading a carriage, believing in the same God and the same religion. He says that the husband needs to take care of the wife. I know that when I get married, he must follow the same religion as me. It makes me feel happy thinking about the kind of family I will have. My husband should go to a Baptist church and believe in the bible. He'll follow what the pastor says and be a good man who takes care of his family and lives a clean life.

In August, Yasmin goes into labor. She calls me. Daddy Mark is going to drive her to the hospital. I have Doug come to get me so he can drive me to the hospital and take care of Tia. When I get to Labor and Delivery, Mama Betty isn't there, so I ask if I can be in the room with Yasmin. I know what it's like to be scared, in pain, and all alone. I won't let that happen to Yasmin. I remind her how to breathe, and we take the breaths together. I hold her hand, knowing how important it is to really feel someone's presence. Yasmin is too little, just fourteen and she's petite anyway, so the baby will not come. The doctor took out a pair of forceps. They are large and scary, but I make Yasmin look at me. I can see the doctor pulling beyond her legs. At Park School, they taught us about forceps, so I know sometimes they're needed, but this is taking way too long, longer than the teachers said it should. Worried, I ask why it's taking so long. The doctor laughs and says, "It's easy going in, but it's hard coming out." I wish I could say I can't believe a man could be so cruel, but I know better.

After an hour, a nine-pound baby girl is born. Yasmin names her Nadia. Her head is shaped like a cone. Yasmin is upset about what they did to her baby's head. But the nurses say we just have to keep molding it. But she is beautiful. And Yasmin is so happy. Over the next three days, Yasmin learns about taking care of her baby. Daddy Mark comes on the day they are discharged, so I don't get to see them go home.

The baby's father tries to help and do stuff. The dad's mother buys diapers, even though she is poor herself. Daddy Mark kicks the father out of the house whenever he sees him, so after a few weeks, Yasmin sneaks Nadia out to see her daddy. Daddy Mark doesn't want her to take the baby out, just like me--maybe he doesn't want people to see that his adoptive daughters are both teen mothers--but she does it anyway. I'm so happy Tia and Nadia will grow up together. I'm heartbroken because I can't see them like I want. Daddy Mark is talking about me like I'm a dog, and Doug tells me what he says when he takes me to work. My feelings are hurt and it's sad that I'm not in college so I can get good grades and make Daddy Mark care about me again or least my grades.

Doug takes me to work so he can take Tia back home to take care of her. When Tia is there, everybody loves her, and she walks and talks and plays with Yasmin and Junior and loves baby Nadia. I feel bad that I'm not there to help Yasmin with Nadia. I miss Tia every minute and wish I could be the one changing her diapers, playing with her, and rocking her to sleep. When school starts again, Yasmin still goes to Park School, and she puts Nadia in their daycare center.

One day when Doug takes me home from work, he says, "You know, Tia saved Nadia's life."

"What do you mean?" I ask. I'm scared that something bad has happened to Nadia and Yasmin.

"You know how hard Yasmin sleeps? She fell asleep and rolled over onto Nadia. Tia came downstairs and told Papa, 'Bon, Bon!' He didn't know what she was saying, but he followed her upstairs and found Yasmin on top of Nadia. He yelled and cussed her out, but Nadia is safe." Doug is clearly proud of our fifteen-month-old daughter. There are times when I think he cares, like he might be a good father.

I am proud of Tia for so many things. She is already potty trained at eighteen months. It took me just two weeks because I followed the guidelines in *Parents* magazine. I am proud of myself, too. Even in this pest-infested apartment, I am going to be a good mom.

We have our first Christmas alone in the apartment. Tia is going to have Christmas every year, and it is going to be wonderful. I went to Kmart and got a tree in a box with some lights and ornaments. I buy all the toys I can afford that are appropriate for her age. There are trucks that a kid can sit on and scoot around. It's hard to decide which one because they are both pretty. I'm surprised when I tell myself, "I don't have to decide. I'm getting them both." That is the day I know I am going to spoil my daughter. I don't care--she is going to have a life different from mine in every way. She is never going to know what it feels like to not have a Christmas.

In my apartment, I know it's a bad neighborhood. There are roaches in the apartment, and I can hear rats in the ceiling when Tia and I go to bed. I have heard that rats will bite your baby, so Tia and I start sleeping together in the hideaway bed. Doug tells me that Daddy Mark says I'm not going to amount to nothing because I live in a rat and roach place. I don't go to their house, and I really miss Yasmin and Junior. I'm sad that we won't spend Christmas together.

The living room is crowded because we have the bed open in there. I put the tree in Tia's room since her window faces the street. She helps me put the ornaments on the tree. A feeling of total happiness overtakes me. I have the life that I want. We can be happy here for now. Despite the many pests, I still feel freer and happier than I ever have.

I decided the last straw for my apartment is when I wake up in the middle of the night hearing a woman screaming in the alley. I pulled Tia close to me, scared and not knowing what to do. I can hear sirens wailing but it seems like it takes a long time, and the screaming goes on and on. I call my landlord the next day and tell him I need to move. I need to keep Tia safe.

My second apartment is in a better place, closer to Yasmin and Junior, which is good because since I left, they have been beaten more, and even though Daddy Mark still gets money for them, and he's even still collecting money for me until I turn 18, he doesn't spend it on them. They didn't have decent clothes or shoes.

He could have given me money for a couch or to cover some of my costs from the money he got from the state, but he didn't give me money for anything. I give my siblings money and buy them little things when I can, but it will be good to be closer. Now, they can walk to my apartment. The apartment is only $185 but it's smaller, only one bedroom. I live so close; Doug sneaks over to see me at night on occasion. He says he wants to buy a stereo for my apartment so he can have his music when he comes. But not here that often. I guess he wants to have something here that his as if Tia isn't. What about the control he has over me? He does pays for cable so Tia and I can have television. He also gives me $50 sometimes to help take care of Tia. People come to visit my nice little apartment. I'm not lonely, I have money for groceries, rent, and to buy stuff. I'm loving my life right now.

After I lived here on my own for about six months, I found myself feeling less and less afraid of Daddy Mark. My birthday is approaching, and I remember my vow after Daddy

Mark beat me that I would see my dad when I turn eighteen. My real daddy has said I need to wait until I'm eighteen so nobody can stop me. He says he will send me money to come visit him in Jackson. Just me and Tia are going, and I pack our bags excitedly for the three days we will be staying. Daddy Mark still won't let Yasmin and Junior go to see Daddy--he won't even let them come to my apartment. When I unpacked, I realized I forgot my pills and I won't have them for three days. I think that's probably okay, and I have more important things to worry about on this trip. I want to make sure Daddy gets to know and love Tia, and that he loves me. Somewhere deep inside I need to know that my daddy loves me as much as he loves the kids he's actually raising.

He's angry at me for having Tia. He holds her and talks to her, making her laugh, even though he says she looks like Doug's mom. He doesn't say anything about how Doug got me pregnant in that place, the place where his kids were taken away too. Probably he and Vanessa talked about it, but he didn't say anything to me. Vanessa doesn't try to get close to me or Tia, but I don't care about that. She isn't motherly, even to her own kids. Even though it's my birthday, I remember that Daddy thinks the white man commercialized birthdays and holidays, so I know I won't get any gifts or cake. I don't care because I'm so happy to be with him. If he gets to know me and Tia better after all these years, he will have to love us. We are blood, daddy and me and Tia, just like Doug and me and Tia are now. You have to love your family because like Mama Betty says, blood is thicker than water. I want to be linked to someone by something more than money from the state. I want to be linked by blood.

When I get back, Doug is waiting for me. He picks me up from the bus station and takes me to my apartment. He tells me how much he missed me and how much he wants me. I can't say no to him because I owe him for picking me and Tia up from the bus station. He walks me into the apartment and Tia goes to sleep. Doug is in a hurry--he always has limited time--so he's quick about it, but he gets what he wants. I start up my pills right away and take extra to make up for the days I missed. I need to make sure that when Doug pressures me for sex, I'm not risking getting pregnant again. I hate pills, but at Park School they said we really have to take them, so we don't get pregnant again. Doug isn't allowed to come to my apartment often, but I need to be prepared when he can sneak away and make demands. My period dwindles but I think that is because of the Pill. By April, no period. I go see my doctor, who says I'm pregnant and I'll probably have a child with disabilities because I had been taking the Pill the whole first trimester. The doctor wants to set me up with counseling so I will be prepared to raise a baby with challenges when that happens. I'm scared and I don't know how I will do everything by myself. After he finds out, Doug goes out and buys that stereo he wants. It's like a slap in the face. It's clear he isn't taking being a father seriously.

The baby miscarried three weeks later on May 11. Right after Tia's second birthday in April. I tell Rennie, who's still my best friend, and Taylor, and I cry on their shoulders. We all feel bad, but I also feel relief. I am just making it with Tia and myself. I don't think I could have made it with another baby, especially one with disabilities. I would have had to give him/her up for adoption. That would have been worst, I think.

Chapter 20

Brighter and Brighter

The beautiful thing about learning is that no one can take it away from you."
— B.B. King, jazz musician

Despite everything, this is the happiest summer of my life. Life with Tia feels perfect. The one bedroom has enough room for my bed and Tia's crib. Every night I fall asleep to the sound of her breathing, and that rhythm directs my heartbeat. I live in an old house that has been converted to three apartments, mine on the first floor. It is at the back of the house facing the alley, which isn't pretty, but it's better than the last place. The apartment has an alcove, which is my favorite place in the world. I put our green couch there, and the window looking outside toward the alley has a view of the trees in the backyard. The bathroom is so small there is only a standup shower--I had never seen one before. I have to put Tia's baby tub in the shower and fill it with warm water. Squatting on my knees, I play with Tia, splashing and laughing.

My little apartment becomes the spot for my family and friends. Rennie and her cousin Jill came to hang out. Jill has always been more like a sister to Rennie, and she and I are becoming better friends, too. Sometimes when Tia is with Doug and Mama Betty, we walk to the Savoy to see a movie, just like before. Taylor, who lived with me for a while and then rented the apartment upstairs, comes to hang out, too. After becoming successful at the Post Office, Taylor's mom moved them to an upscale neighborhood. Her parents got divorced, and Taylor rebelled against her mom, so as soon as she turned eighteen, she decided to move out. She wants to have the freedom to see men if she wants, and to party and have fun. It's fun having her around, but I don't have that kind of life. I still have to work at the nursing home and take care of Tia. There's a new male aide, and it's pretty rare for a man to work with us, so he is attracting a lot of attention. He acts like he likes me.

After a couple of months, the new male aide appears to still like me. All the girls like him, but I remind myself that I am the kind of girl who doesn't like the guy everyone else likes—I don't like the feeling of competition. I learned that from when Taylor liked Ryder. So, while the other girls giggle and try to start conversations, I just go about my work.

"I really want to take you out," Ryan says, stopping me in the hallway as I push a linen cart from room to room. My job today is to make all the beds up.

"But you have all these girls interested in you," I say, trying to hide my surprise, not sure if it comes off as indifference.

"I really want to take you out," he says again. He is persistent. I let him know I am a teenage mother with a toddler at home. I let him know about Doug, though I don't tell Doug about him. Doug and I aren't actually dating, we are just parenting together (whatever parenting he didn't get to lay off on his mother), but I rely on him to make sure Tia is taken care of while I'm at work, so I can't afford to make Doug or his mother angry.

Ryan's interest turns out to be irresistible, though. I started to like him because he seems so different from most of the guys I know. I mostly have poor comparisons to make with Doug, since most of the other men I have encountered in my life have been awful in some way—in many ways. Ryan manages to convince me that he really likes me for me, and I start to like him, too. He says things like, "I admire you; you work full time while raising a daughter alone at only 18."

This has been going on for a few months, so I agree on a date, and one day while Tia is with Doug, I get into Ryan's car, and we drive to Lake Michigan. All those years living less than an hour's drive away from this magnificent place, and I had never gone. I hadn't even known that we lived that close to the lake. The last time I was near a body of water like this was a brief look at Niagara Falls when Daddy to us to Buffalo.

It's late June now, and the air is cool, but the sun in the blue sky is white and blinding. I feel a sense of wonder knowing that this is the only sun on earth, the same sun I see in Grand Rapids, the same sun everybody sees. The waves rush over the sandy shoreline in a rhythm that almost makes me want to dance. I find myself swaying next to Ryan, watching the deep blue spread across the horizon as far as I can see. I can't say anything because I'm in awe. The gulls and the rushing of the waves are the only sounds, until I hear Ryan breathing next to me. There is so much in the world that I don't know about, and I realize that my education is the only way I will ever experience more than just a small part of it.

And I fell in love—with the lake and with Ryan. Ryan says I haven't seen anything, yet. He wants me to see the sunset. We sit on a blanket on the beach and talk. I have never seen anything so beautiful in my life as the sight of the sun sinking into the lake, the sky amazing blues and pinks and purples. The last trails of light trickle across the water, and then it's dusk. We stopped talking and kissed. It is the first time I know what it feels like to fall in love. The truth is that I don't really know what love is. The waves rush onto the shore and roll away, and the man next to me breathes in and out. I feel content and at peace. I feel like it's okay to be me.

The waves washing toward me and then sliding back into the Great Lake mesmerize me as the sky darkens. The overwhelming beauty of the lake and the quiet serenity of sitting there with no obligations or expectations is calming. I think that if I could spend every day on that beach, I could forget my past life and be happy.

But I have to go back to my life and my apartment, and I can't wait to see Tia. She is spending the night at her daddy's, so I have time for myself to think. I remind myself that I am supposed to love Doug. After all, he's my daughters' father. I'm supposed to. I know what it's like to be taken from your father, and I don't want that for Tia. So far, Doug has been sneaking over sometimes even though Daddy Mark said he wasn't allowed to visit my apartment. Doug is still scared of Daddy Mark, more than me. He still lives there with them. He's coming just to see Tia, and me, I guess. But we aren't dating.

I always wondered what it would be like to date somebody normal. Somebody I could tell people I was dating. Somebody I could actually go out with. I tell myself; *this is how you meet a person--at work or someplace normal. They take you out. They pay for the date. They treat you like you are the most beautiful person.* I think those things as though they can only happen to somebody else. When we were sitting on the beach, Ryan said he fell in love with my smile. He thought I was beautiful and kind. Nobody had ever complimented me like that--like they do in movies. The only thing Doug ever said was that I was knock-kneed. He liked petite women. Since I had Tia, I wasn't petite--I had retained a few pounds. Altogether I had gained 35 pounds when I was pregnant. I had lost 26 but couldn't get off the last 9 pounds. Doug didn't stop reminding me that I wasn't cute enough for him.

I invite Ryan over to meet Tia, and he falls in love with her. He wants to be with me despite all the other crazy things about my life. As I learn more about Ryan, I see how he is different from most of the other men I have known. We date for a few months before we become physically intimate because Ryan wants me to be sure. His caring how I feel is so strange and so beautiful. In my eighteen years, it has never occurred to me that I can ask for and get what I want, that my feelings about anything that happens to me actually matter. At twenty-five, Ryan is older than me, and I think of him as an adult, which is odd because I'm the one with all the responsibilities of an adult. At Park School, the older the man the better—all the girls thought you must be mature, have *all that* if an older man was interested in you. But with Ryan, it's not about being impressive to my friends. He loves me, at least I think he does, but I never know if it's enough. His love is something I want so badly to believe in because I love him, but I can't convince myself that I deserve to be loved. I also know deep down that love seems too impossible and too tainted to be real.

Ryan had graduated from Aquinas College with a major in geography. He chose it because his mom forced him to go to college and he thought geography was the easiest thing to study. Before that, his mom pushed him to be a priest. He is a Catholic, but he doesn't seem to like church. He complains that my church service is so long. But he is so smart and nice. His mom really just wanted him to go to college and get out of the ghetto in Saginaw. She was an overprotective mom, but I can respect that. He's well-suited to the nursing home, though. He is kind and happy, and he cheers the residents. Now that I'm a college student at Davenport College, we have something else in common.

Yasmin and Junior can walk over to my apartment any time with Nadia in her stroller, when Daddy Mark is at work and Mama Betty is out with her sister. Sometimes on my days off, I meet them nearby at Franklin Park, because I can walk Tia in her stroller, and she can play with Yasmin, Junior, and Nadia. It makes me so happy to see them, and it feels like we are a family again.

On the Fourth of July, I realized that I had been on my own for a whole year. I feel pride that I did it, made it on my own with Tia, my own life, my own job, my own money. And I have Ryan. Taylor is staying with me this month because her mom wants to see if Taylor can be on her own, like me. Her mom is proud of me, and that makes me feel good. Taylor, Tia, and I go out on the streets to see the fireworks, and it's like a big party on Franklin and Eastern—inside I am celebrating for myself and Tia while everybody else is celebrating Independence Day. I give Tia a sparkler and she likes it. All over the neighborhood, people are out lighting off bottle rockets and M-80s. Tia might be too young for all of the loud bangs at just two years old. She is afraid of all the lights and noise, so we have to go in, but I still feel like I got *my* celebration.

In September, Ryan takes me to the fireworks for the City of Grand Rapids. We spread our blanket on a hill at Ah-Nab-Awen Park downtown. Everyone around us is happy and having fun. I'm happy, too, sitting there with Ryan and Tia, feeling like my life is going the way that I want it to go. I have somebody who cares about me enough to take me out and to share this with me and Tia. We're excited to see the fireworks, though I'm not sure Tia, at age two, will be okay this time. When the fireworks go off, she cries, but everything is so exciting and wonderful that I don't want to leave, so I hug her to my chest, and she calms and falls asleep. Ryan has his camera and is taking pictures of the crowd, of us, of the sky as it lights up with one spectacular boom after another.

Later that summer, Doug saw a notice and said I should take the test for the post office. They pay well and the work is steady. Taylor's mom is a post office worker, and she does pretty well, but I can't help thinking that it's kind of like factory work. If I get to work there, I will risk losing the job and not being able to find a new one to keep the same wages. I took the test just in case, and I scored really well. It's mostly numerical questions, and I like that. A representative contacted me about taking the job and I am thinking about it, but I know the post office isn't my dream. Something inside me says I can do more, that somehow, I *am* going to do more. I just need to find a way.

I still think sometimes about being a teacher. Whenever I can, I teach Tia her colors, letters, and numbers, just like I did with Yasmin and Junior. Then the news comes out that teachers are getting pink slips--that means they are losing their jobs. I can't afford to take a job that I might lose now that Tia is depending on me. One day in the mail, I got a flyer from Davenport College. They say they have financial aid, and they will work around your schedule. There is a double major in accounting, which is math, so I know I will love it, combined with a major in computers. I say, "I'm going to major in that because I think those computers are going to take over the world." The only one there to hear me is Tia, but I hope this is the right decision.

It's like a new world opening in my mind. I might be able to do this, might be able to go to college and fulfill my dreams. It's hard to squash down the doubt and questions. I tell myself I already know I can work full-time, go to school, and take care of Tia. I did that already when I was in high school. I call the number on the brochure to make an appointment with a counselor. I hope she is just as helpful as Mrs. Brown was.

When I go in for the appointment, I must walk into the big administrative building. Tia is with me, and she is behaving like a good girl. There are students walking around, looking like they know what they are doing. Only a few looked like me. The floors are marble, and there are columns in front of the big reception desk. I am sent to the counselor's office. She is impressed by my grades, and by the fact that I had a daughter and still graduated early. I have the brochure with me and ask, "How can I get this degree?" I point to where it says I can earn accounting and computer programming degrees combined. I want to make sure I can learn what I need to learn to get a good job—I don't have time to do anything extra. Tia is curious, looking around at everything. I picked her up to go but the guidance counselor told me I can enroll right away, so she sent me to the financial aid office.

When I go to the financial aid office, I am sent to the office of Marianne Bethune. Marianne sees Tia and takes her into her lap. She tells me that I can get a scholarship and financial aid to pay for college. I can't believe that I will be able to go. It's almost like she's my fairy godmother, in a world where a fairy godmother has never appeared before. Since I live on my own and I have my own tax returns, I don't have to ask Mama Betty or Daddy Mark for anything. When Mrs. Bethune tells me this, I am so relieved. I don't know how, but I think that if they were able, Mama Betty and Daddy Mark might do something to stop me—that is how mad at me Daddy Mark is. Daddy Mark had been telling everybody that I wasn't going to amount to nothing. I am going to prove that he is wrong about me.

I can't stop smiling when I get home. In a month, I am going to be a college student. And in two years, I am going to be a college graduate, with a double major associate degree. As I go to work at the nursing home, I think that maybe I won't be doing this forever.

When the schedule for my first trimester arrives in the mail, I feel like I'm holding a treasure in that small envelope. It hits me like a wave of joy that I am really going to college. I have been tested out of the computer typing class because of my experience in high school—that's four credits, which means I'm really a college student. Taking the test was nerve wracking, but I made myself concentrate and show what I am capable of. It's a good sign, I think, for my first trimester.

After I get the schedule and my book vouchers, I take a bus downtown to the campus to buy my books before the trimester starts. Marianne has helped me get the money I need so I can pay for all my school expenses, which is good because I just earn enough money at the nursing home to pay the bills for me and Tia. I take the bus to Davenport and when I step off and stand in front of the building, I think *I am looking at my future.* On the way back, I have to carry a heavy bag of books, the weight reminding me of how important my education is. I have an accounting book, data processing book, and a math book. It's exciting to me just to hold them and flip through the pages. This is the happiest I have been in my life besides giving birth to Tia.

I feel a little scared as I approach the Davenport building for my first day. I'm really starting college on time because I'm eighteen, but the kids here seem so much younger than me, and I'm not sure how I will fit in. My schedule shows the numbers of the section--but I'm not sure where to go. I try not to show my nerves as I decode the information and find my classroom. I sit at a chair at a table in the front of the room. I'm too nervous to talk--that isn't like me. Looking around without seeming like I'm looking around; I see other students; maybe they're nervous too. It's early in the morning, so a lot of them look tired. It's good that I'm a morning person because I have to schedule classes so I can make it to the nursing home on days I'm working. After a few minutes, I realized this is a lot like high school. Students sit at desks and a teacher stands at the front and teaches. That makes me feel better. Can anyone tell I am a parent? That's where I am different.

I love everything about this. I love learning about what a syllabus is when the professor passes it out. It tells me everything that is going to happen in the class and what the expectations are. That's when it hits me: *I can do this. I'm going to do this.* I listen and take notes, then between classes, I sit in the cafeteria and read the book for my next class so I will know what the professor is talking about.

For my first day of college, I don't have to go to work afterward, so Doug meets me with Tia when I get home. I'm so excited to talk about my day, telling him about the classes, the teachers, the way the building felt when I first walked in. Doug doesn't say anything. He's always teased me about being smart and talking white. I wonder if he's jealous, since he dropped out of Key 5 Institute, and I'm going to a real college. I try not to feel disappointed, and when he leaves, I play with Tia and tell her about my day. A two-year-old might not understand college, but she can be happy with me.

One of the odd side effects of going to college is that both Ryan and I have white friends from school—after all that's mostly who is going to college. I liked the fact that Ryan is black with white friends because then he could understand me—he didn't tease me about the way I talked or because I was smart. There are only two other black people in my program at Davenport, a man who is also majoring in accounting and a woman named Sara from Bangor—she is well off and sounds white, whiter than me, though there is nobody to tease us about it. I actually love being someplace where people don't mention or care about how I talk.

The biggest thing that I notice is that everybody there is a regular teenager. Sara and some of the other kids live in a dorm. They have parents who still take care of them, and they go out and have fun when they aren't studying. I am a little jealous that I can't have all of that. But I try to focus on what I do have and be happy about that. All the time I remind myself that I am building a life for myself. Sarah seems amazed that I live on my own and I'm a mother. She's nice to me, even though we are different. I like feeling like I have the same opportunities that these other students have.

I meet Ryan's best friend James when we go to a bar once, and we often go out with other friends. I don't feel too uncomfortable because everyone around me is friendly yet white. However, I do feel a little uncomfortable because they are all at least seven years older than me and they have graduated and are living their lives. One of Ryan's other friends Tim gets drunk and obnoxious. But when things get out of control Ryan always respects me enough to leave if I want to. Ryan and I can compare notes on how white people are different from us. All of Ryan's friends are white, and I find out that all of his past girlfriends have been white, too. I wonder if he can really love me, a black woman.

When they get together, James and Ryan like to drink-- they are still living the 'college life' in a lot of ways. I don't usually drink, but once in a while, Ryan gives me a few, then laughs about what a lightweight I am. We toast that I'm headed to college. Ryan is so happy for me and proud, too.

My first trimester of college at Davenport is going very well and I didn't know I could be this happy. In Intro to Data Processing, we are the first class that will be learning Basic programming without punch cards. First the professor taught programming using punch cards. This means sitting at an IBM card punch machine with a stack of cream colored eight-inch by three-inch cards. Punch cards had been around since 1890, but IBM introduced their typewriter-like machines in the 1960s

163

and they were used through the 1970s. After we take a card and program it through the machine, we are instructed to put it through the shredders. The professor says, "Now that you know what the past is like, we are going to move into the future. You'll learn how to program using Basic." It is so exciting to know I am on the cusp of a revolution. I diligently learn about programming the if/then statements in Basic. The room is dominated by white males, but this is what I'm used to. I realize I made the right decision in my major--it's clear now that I am going to be at the front of this driving force in the world.

Chapter 21

Love and Love Lost

**"Choose your life's mate closely. From this one decision
will come 90 percent of all your happiness or misery."
—H. Jackson Brown, Jr.**

With everything in my life going well, I decided I
needed to tell Doug about Ryan. Doug is mad. I don't think it's
because he loves me; it's because he feels like he owns me.
Even though I am no longer having a relationship with Doug,
he says things like, "I want you." Which I know in some way
has nothing to do with love and everything to do with control.
That's why he calls me his main squeeze. It's supposed to
make me feel special and good. I feel like he needs me, though,
so I listen to him, not thinking about how our "relationship"
started when I was just a kid. Plus, deep down, I want Doug to
love me so much that I push all those doubts down and make
myself remember that I *love* him. Or was he my teenage crush?
He was one of the first males to talk to me like a friend. Doug
doesn't want anybody else to be Tia's father, and Doug is in
my life, permanently, so I feel tied to him.

Until I met Ryan, romantic love wasn't something I
ever really expected in my life, only hoped. I used to read Judy
Blume books when I was winning the library summer reading
contests, and they made me think about what love was, but I
really didn't understand the whole concept. Like everybody
else, I had seen the movies and heard the stories, but it never
seemed real for me, not the kind of romantic love that might
exist for everybody else.

Regina 18, Tia 2

My days are constant and exhausting work. At this point in my life, I am just surviving—working, going to school, keeping up the apartment, making sure there is food, doing the dishes, spending time with Tia, trying to make sure Junior and Yasmin, and now Nadia, are safe and cared for. I feel like I am failing, especially for Junior, Yasmin, and Nadia because I just can't keep up with everything that is happening to them even now that I don't live as far away from them. Being close to Daddy Mark and Mama Betty's house is one way I can be closer to them, but with my schedule, it's still hard to see them often enough.

Late in October, Daddy Mark comes over to my apartment drunk. He pounds on the door yelling, "Is Doug in there?" It's late and I'm sitting on the couch with Tia watching television. I don't want to answer the door. I hugged Tia closely and hoped that he would leave. Instead, he shoots a gun through the door. The noise is loud, and it makes me jump. Everything slows down, and the world doesn't seem real. My ears echo with the boom of the gun and Tia is crying, but I can barely hear her. We hide at the back of the room. I hold myself over her and wait for more. The door is on the side of the alcove, so the bullets won't come near us, but I don't know what Daddy Mark might do next. He yells, "Stop sleeping with your brother!" and I wonder if someone at the bar said something. There's nothing I can say because he won't believe me if I tell him I'm not sleeping with Doug. Did he say anything to Doug about this? Daddy Mark must hear Tia crying, so he goes away. I am supposed to be on my own, and I won't put up with this. I got up and called the police.

When they get to my apartment, they ask me if I know who did it. I told them it was my adopted father. The officers don't believe me. They ask why he would do something like that. I think I shouldn't tell them that he was looking for Doug, my baby's father and my adopted brother. Even in the hood, this won't sound good. So, I say, "I don't know". The police officers take the report and leave without doing anything.

The next morning, our whole lives change. I hear a knock on the door early in the morning, and when I open it, I see all three of them, Yasmin, Junior, and Nadia. Junior's face is all messed up. He is bloody and his face is swollen. They had waited until Daddy Mark left for work and pretended to walk to school, coming to me instead. They told me that Daddy Mark was having an episode last night. Junior and his best friend David and Yasmin were in the basement when Daddy Mark came home from my apartment. Junior had called Shay a monkey, something he did all the time. Mama Betty beat him, but when Daddy Mark came home, she told him about Junior. David was told to leave immediately. Daddy Mark pistol whipped Junior with the same gun he shot through my apartment. The cuts from the holster of the gun are clear on Junior's face.

I know the police aren't going to want to come back to my apartment after last night. I pack up all of us and we take the bus to the police station. I'm scared. Even though there were beatings while Daddy Mark and Mama Betty were our "parents," we had some stability. Yet, my little brother got the worst beating a boy could have. And I have been shot at again. The second attempt by a "father" to kill me.

I tell the officers my brother had been abused, and they sit us down with a police officer. Junior and Yasmin tell everything that has happened. It's worse than I thought; the abuse has gotten more brutal since I left. I tell the police officer to look up the report from last night to prove that Daddy Mark had the gun he beat Junior with. The officer says that Yasmin, Junior, and Nadia can't go back to that house. I say I know that they will live with me. The officer says they have to go to Child Haven. That's where orphans and children who are abused by their parents go. I stay with them, and we cry. Junior gets cleaned up. When the social worker comes, they cling to me and I don't want to leave them, so I go with them to Child Haven and see them settle in.

I cry the whole time, thinking my brother and sister have to stay here because they have no parents. *They have no parents.* I don't want them to ever go to another foster care home. I have always tried to take care of them, and I am going to figure out a way now. At least Nadia gets to stay with Yasmin. Child-Haven is better than a foster home, but not much. There's security and I can't go back with them to their rooms. They're allowed to come out and say goodbye to me. We all cried some more, and Yasmin and Junior said they wanted to come with me. I can barely walk away; I am crying so hard. Sadness, frustration, and anger well up inside me until I feel like that is all I am made of—a giant pit of emotions. It takes every ounce of my will to take each step that brings me through the door and into the parking lot. Tia and I headed to the bus stop.

Visiting them in that orphanage is one of the hardest things I have ever had to do. It feels worse than when the social worker took me to a separate foster home when we became wards of the state. This place has locks on all the doors. They have to share rooms with other kids in the same situation, more people they don't know. Daddy is in Jackson with his new family, and I have to figure out how I'm going to call and tell him. I'm scared to tell him. We don't have a mother to turn to. She is wherever. I am the only constant in their lives. And now we have two more people to take care of, Nadia and Tia. They're all locked up, and it feels like they're in jail for something they didn't do. They don't deserve this.

When is bad stuff going to stop happening to us? They're only fifteen and sixteen. And possibly headed to another foster home. But not if I can help it. No way. I have to figure out how I can take care of them. Of us. Of all of us. I know I am only eighteen, but I have to try something. They are not going to live here, and they certainly are not going back to the Carpenters. I remember how I told the first social worker that Yasmin and Junior weren't treated right there. They were being abused. And in time things got worse. I hate Daddy Mark

and Mama Betty. Especially Daddy Mark. I always think about
how they adopted us for the money. Even Doug said so. What
is Daddy Mark going to do now? Is it the end of the money
train? What will they be willing to do to talk their way out of
this to keep getting that money? Will they deny everything?
The beatings? The shooting? This time, I have proof. All my
reading of Nancy Drew and the Hardy Boys had taught me that
in order to get justice you need proof. I feel almost excited just
thinking that this time, I have proof. Justice is going to be on
my side.

When I get back to my apartment, I tell the landlord
that there's a bullet hole in the door, and he takes care of it. He
is really nice, knowing I'm a teenage mother and I pay my rent
on time. He asks if I'm okay, and I tell him I'm fine. One more
lie to a stranger; one more lie to me.

We get assigned a caseworker. I must make her
understand that I need to be with Yasmin, Junior, and Nadia.
The caseworker says they will probably go to another foster
home, but I tell her there is no way that can happen. She tells
me that I must get a bigger place to even be considered.

I love my apartment with one bedroom, the alcove, and
the cozy living room. But I have to get a bigger apartment so
they can move in with me. I tell my landlord that I am maybe
getting custody of my brother and sister, so I need more
bedrooms. He finds an apartment that we can move to and
transfer my lease. The rent is more than double what I was
paying. I call my dad, even though I am afraid he will kill
Daddy Mark.

Daddy sends money for the deposit and buys us a new
refrigerator. He drives out to deliver the refrigerator, and I'm
so happy to see him. Since my birthday, I have seen him a
couple of times, and we talk on the phone, but soon will be the
first time he has seen Yasmin and Junior since they were little.
Daddy is so happy that we'll all three be together again and we
are away from Daddy Mark. Daddy had become an ordained
minister, and even though I don't think he can forgive Daddy
Mark, he doesn't confront him. Plus, his time in prison might
have taught him that he sometimes had to let things go. I can't
even tell the caseworker that Daddy is helping us. They still
say he isn't our father, and I'm afraid of what it will mean if

anyone finds out Yasmin and Junior might have contact with him. Would they decide Yasmin and Junior can't come to live with me?

The judge still must decide. In the meantime, we are instructed to go to family counseling. I dread the first counseling session. The caseworker makes us sit down with Daddy Mark and Mama Betty at Child Haven. Daddy Mark and Mama Betty act like they are the best parents in the world. The goal is to have Yasmin, Junior, and Nadia go back with Daddy Mark and Betty. I say there is no way that will happen. My siblings will return to that home over my dead body. The therapist asks, "Regina why do you feel you can handle the care of your daughter, your sister, brother, and niece at only eighteen years old? And you're in college, correct?"

"I've been their parent since my biological mother left thirteen years ago. We belong together, period." I'm not even scared looking at Daddy Mark across the table. All I feel is hate. I even feel hate for Doug, who is such a wimp that he stayed away as instructed by his father. Yasmin and Junior say they are treated well at Child Haven, but I want them to be able to stay with me. After a few weeks, I am told they can stay temporarily, but it won't be permanent unless a judge decides.

Every day, I make sure they go to school and do their homework. I tell them all the time how important school is. Yasmin goes to Park School, and Nadia goes to daycare there. Junior goes to Ottawa Hills High School. They tell me that they didn't get to school all the time with Daddy Mark and Betty. They didn't want to give Yasmin and Junior money for the bus, so Yasmin and Junior would take back bottles to get bus money and leave for school after Daddy Mark and Mama Betty went to work. I'd give them money whenever I could back then.

During the month they live with me, Yasmin gets straight A's in school. Junior goes every day, and he will graduate on time. Eventually, we must go to court and tell a judge what we want. I am scared about talking in front of a courtroom, but my determination to make sure Yasmin, Nadia, and Junior never have to go back to that house is stronger than my fear. The courtroom is more like a small conference room. We sit on one side, and Daddy Mark and Mama Betty sit on the other, and we are looking at each other across the courtroom. Normally I am very scared of Daddy Mark but not now, I just want to hurt him. I want to say I can't believe he did it. Actually, I can. He was always mean as hell, though he pretended to everyone else that he was the great parent who took in three poor children who didn't know love. If he did love us, he had a terrible way of showing it.

At least now the State believes me. He was abusing my siblings all along. No more pretending. I am worried they will try to say that Yasmin and Junior deserved it. I think that nobody deserves this, but then life has never been about what we deserve. All our lives, every adult we encountered had let us down. Adults always win because everyone believes them and not us. But this time, I'm an adult too, and I'm going to win. I am finally going to be believed. The court is going to listen to me. I feel overwhelmed with emotion thinking that I will be able to fight for my family and win so far. The anger makes me strong and determined. Tears collect in the corners of my eyes, and I fight them back so my words will be clear when I have to speak.

Daddy Mark and Mama Betty promise that they will be better. They say they will send the kids to school every day. They will not be physical with them. The caseworker tells the judge that Yasmin and Junior are doing better in school in my temporary custody in just a few months than they did all the time they were living with Daddy Mark and Mama Betty. And that I was setting an example by going to college. The judge asks Yasmin and Junior if they want to return to Daddy Mark and Mama Betty. "No way," they say. "We don't want to go back."

Then the judge asked me 'Did I have anything to say?" I could only say, I love my brother and sister, and I am tired of them being mistreated. Which is why I moved into an apartment big enough for all of us. And I'm making sure they get to school. So please let them continue to stay with me. Please your honor.

The judge looks me in the eyes and says, "You can become their foster mother, and we'll revisit this in one year. Your assigned social worker will make monthly visitations during the year." I look up and say silently Thank you, Jesus. Prayers answered but still surprised, something went my way. I was awarded custody of my siblings. Not only do they not have to go back to Daddy Mark and Mama Betty, but we get to have more days together like the ones we have been having these past couples of months. All of us together, waking up for breakfast, talking, and laughing. It's just like being a family in the way I always dreamed of. And we get to keep doing it. I don't care if a social worker will come to check on us every month. I will fill out all of their paperwork and do whatever I have to make this stick.

I am so angry that Daddy Mark and Mama Betty tried to get Yasmin and Junior back. I don't know what to say to them, and I don't know what I would have done if the judge gave Yasmin and Junior back. I walked out of the courtroom with them feeling triumphant. I want to shout, "You don't have any power over me anymore or by siblings." But I don't.

It's getting cold outside. I take Yasmin and Junior to Sears excited to use my new credit card and get them winter coats and boots. They didn't even have decent shoes to wear to school or warm clothes for the winter. I know that when we were growing up in Daddy Mark and Mama Betty's house that things weren't right, but now I see how bad they were, and I want to make sure I do what I can to make it up to Yasmin and Junior. They are excited to have new clothes to wear, and even more excited because we all get our own bedrooms; it's the first time for them.

For the first time in a long time, we are all together and we don't have to wake up and be scared. Along with the money I earn from working part-time at the nursing home, I get foster care payments and food stamps instead of Daddy Mark, so we can eat what we want and pay the rent and utilities. By mid-winter, I barely have enough money because our gas bill is so high, but somehow, we make it, and we don't get utilities cut off. Doing all this is exhausting because I am still at Davenport full-time, but it is worth it and even more important now because I have my family, the family that matters.

Even before I finish my first trimester, I start planning for the next trimester. This means registering for classes, getting my new schedule, and seeing Mrs. Bethune of Financial Aid to get my book vouchers. I told her all about what has happened with Yasmin and Junior coming to live with me. My foster care income must be included in my new financial aid. But then so does my family size. So, I'll be alright.

Marianne says, "Wow, how are you going to be able to continue school?"

"I don't know, but I'm not dropping out. I am going to get my degree," I say. She just shakes her head. Then she helps me to make sure that I get what I need. I register for another accounting class, College English 1, Principles of COBOL, and Intro to Business. She tells me to come back if I need anything, and I learned then she is a person I can count on.

Ryan sticks by my side. He wakes up every morning and picks me up at 5:30 a.m. for our 6 a.m. to 2:30 p.m. shift. Even though that means crossing paths with Doug who comes to pick up Tia and take her back to his mother's, before Yasmin and Junior get on the bus to school. Ryan is always there to talk me through the stress, but I am so tired so much of the time.

When I meet his mother, she tells me that she doesn't want her son tied down to a woman with kids to raise. She thinks it is too much to ask of him. I wonder if she is right, but I don't think Ryan is going to marry me or anything, so I'm not sure why she is telling me this. I just want to enjoy being together and have someone in my life who supports me. I want to enjoy the time we have together. I try not to be a burden on Ryan, and I think we will have a pretty good time together. He's there for a lot of my daily life, but he has a separate life, too.

Thanksgiving that year was the best time we have ever had. Tia is two years old; Nadia is one, and they love each other so much. It's just Yasmin, Junior, me, and the babies. We are all in the kitchen together. I cook everything I know how to cook. I teach Yasmin and Junior how to bake cookies. We play music and dance and laugh together all day. Even going to the grocery store is wonderful. We are going to make a sweet potato pie. Nutmeg is an ingredient, but it is so expensive, $4 for such a little item, and it's more than milk and bread put together. Before I know it, I slip the little bottle in my purse. Yasmin and Junior look at me with wide eyes--nobody would ever believe that I would do something bad. I tell them, "Don't ever do anything like this." But having the perfect Thanksgiving together is more important than anything right now, so I am willing to do something bad. We enjoy every part of that meal, and all say we are thankful that we are together.

On Saturday mornings, I wake up and make a big breakfast for everyone. We can't do that on weekdays because we are always rushing off to work and school. It's nice to have time to sit together and talk before we start our day. When we are clearing the plates, Yasmin rushes out of the room. We can hear her throwing up in the bathroom, and Junior and I look at each other. When she comes back in, I ask her, "Are you pregnant?" It turns out that she got pregnant before they went to Child Haven. I try not to show it, but I'm scared. Will a caseworker use this as an excuse to take us apart? We have a new caseworker now. He is short with red curly hair and seems nice enough, but I know better than to trust. Junior says, "Damn, now they are going to break us up." Yasmin is just fifteen. But once I tell him, the caseworker tries to talk Yasmin into giving her baby up for adoption. I tell her not to, we will take care of her. She agrees with the caseworker, just to make sure he doesn't take her away. The caseworker doesn't break us up, at least for now.

Christmas is even better than Thanksgiving. I use my credit card to buy presents. I give Yasmin money I saved so she can get Nadia presents on her own, but I make sure Tia and Nadia have the same number of presents. And I don't want either of them to ever feel less loved and less important than the other. I know how that chip away at your soul. Yasmin and Junior and I all got presents for each other. The most fun is decorating the tree and the apartment. I have some extra time because school is on Christmas break. We play cards and Monopoly at night and plan what we will have for Christmas dinner. I am so excited that I can make this day special for everyone in a way we have never had before. Our front window looks out over an empty lot on Michigan and College Street, and I make sure that the lights from the tree sparkle so anyone going by can see them. We make up little bags of fruit and candy, just like we learned to at Daddy Mark and Betty's, but ours are decorated to look special.

After Christmas, we have a run of birthdays, mine in January, Yasmin's in February, and Junior's in March. Right before my birthday, I get my college grades in the mail. When the envelope comes in the mail, I am nervous. I know I tried my best, but a lot has happened during this term, and it was so hard to handle all of the family trauma and keep up with four classes. I finally opened the envelope, and it's like a gift to myself. I got two A's, in Accounting I and College Reading, and two B's in Intro to Data Processing and Business Math. When I celebrate my birthday, I'm also celebrating the first step in my dream to finish my education.

After having a birthday cake for my seventeenth birthday, I had to skip a year because I was at Daddy's for my eighteenth birthday, but this year, I'm having chocolate on chocolate cake, and I made it myself in *my* kitchen with my siblings' help. We give the spoons to Tia and Nadia after we mix the frosting. It is one of those rare moments when everything feels so unexpectedly wonderful that I know I am going to be okay. Right? Like Grandmo said.

It's even more fun celebrating Yasmin's and Junior's birthdays since they are the first birthday cakes, I can remember them ever having. I made Yasmin, a yellow cake with chocolate frosting. I light sixteen candles, and we sing "Happy Birthday" loudly and with immense joy. I want to make her Sweet Sixteen special even though she is five months pregnant. I don't want her to feel the way I felt, so we focus on happy things. The only thing that matters is we are celebrating together.

We will soon celebrate Junior's birthday, too. Junior doesn't want a traditional cake, though. He wants cheesecake, his favorite sweet. So, I buy three boxes of Ready-Made Cheesecake and a gallon of milk, even though it costs a lot of money, and make him the largest cheesecake we've ever seen in my 13 x 9-inch pan. It looks so good. He just beamed at the sight of it. I say, "Okay, we have to sing and blow out the candle." I had only put one on it because I was afraid seventeen candles would melt the cheesecake. He pauses over the lit candle as we sing with tears welling in his eyes--he doesn't want to eat it just yet. We all hugged, and I said, "Go ahead," to encourage him. Junior blows out the candle and I hope his wishes come true.

Chapter 22

I Am So Tired

**"Freeing yourself is one thing. Claiming ownership of that
freed self is another."
—Toni Morrison**

The end of March also means the end of the second trimester at Davenport. I try not to be unhappy about my grades. Doing everything to work and take care of everybody had been so hard. I knew all along that I wasn't going to give up, but it's kind of disappointing that I earned two B's and two C's. The B's are in Accounting II and College English and the C's in my COBOL and Intro to Business classes. I think about how the C's replaced the A's I'd gotten the first term. Life is more difficult than I expected when I started college. But I am not giving up. One day, I vow, I will not need the state's foster care payments to feed and clothe my family. More is at stake now. I must get Junior and Yasmin through high school. That's another year away. So, I enrolled into the third and last term of my first year of college, taking Accounting III, Principles of RPG, and Interpersonal Communications. Three classes is still full time, but I hope it will be more manageable than the four I have been taking.

Our run of birthdays continues with Tia's third birthday in April. We have a big party right there in our apartment--just us. Rennie's mother, who is Tia's godmother, stops by to drop off a gift. Rennie's mother is a real godmother, checking in on us from time to time. One time when she stopped by, Tia and I had just finished playing with her hair box. It was something she loved to do. I was laying on the couch letting her put every barrette and tie in my hair. It was so embarrassing to have Ma Doris find me like that, but she just laughed. Daddy Mark and Mama Betty never checked on us— they only had contact with Tia when she went over there while I worked. Maybe they had their own birthday celebration for her with Doug.

One day soon after Tia's birthday Doug is running late, so I have to leave her with Yasmin and Junior when Ryan gets there to pick me up for work. Everyone is still asleep because it's just 5:30 in the morning, but I know Doug will get there soon. Ryan lightly honks his horn like he usually does, and I kiss Tia goodbye. She wakes up and says, "Mommy, don't leave." It feels like I have no choice; I have to go to work, and Ryan is waiting. When I get to his car, I look up to her bedroom window, and I see Tia there crying. She is so small and fragile, just a little younger than I was when *she* left me.

"I can't go to work," I say to Ryan. He says Tia will be fine and that Doug will be there soon to take her.

"You have to go to work. If you don't, you'll lose your job." Ryan is trying to be supportive, I guess, but it just makes me angry. I can't put my job above Tia. Nothing is more important than her. So, I let Ryan drive away, at that moment I think should I finally accept Doug's marriage proposal. I think about what Ryan's mom told me—that I would be a burden to him with all of my family to support. I wonder if I have been fair to him, asking him to do so much when he could be with someone who didn't have a child and two siblings to take care of. Daddy Mark always said, "Once you have a kid, nobody will want to marry you."

I want so much to have someone love me. Between Ryan and Doug, I have been wondering who will love me more, who will take care of me, who will help me, so I won't be so tired. Whoever loves me, I could then make up my mind to really *love* him if I don't already. To love him the best that I can. People say if you have never been loved, you don't know how to love. I say, I know how to love. I love my brother and sister and niece and nephew. I love Tia more than anything in the world.

I want Tia to have her father. And I am tired. Doug has been pressuring me to marry him and I have resisted, feeling that my relationship with Ryan was getting stronger. But I am tired. I believe I do love Ryan, but I can't believe he loves me like that. Why should he? I carry a lot with me. Even though he really acts like he loves my family, he hasn't shown me any signs that he is thinking of marrying me. I walk back upstairs to my apartment and grab Tia and hug her. When Doug gets there to pick her up, I tell him that I will marry him. At first, I just felt relief. Then I wonder if I am doing the right thing because of Ryan. My foremost thought is that I am giving my daughter her father. She will grow up in a family with her real father.

And I am so tired. Doug doesn't really react, but he asks if, I am sure. I said yes, and he said OKAY.

I don't know how I can tell Ryan. I don't have to see him until the next day when he comes to pick me up for work. When he gets there, Doug's car—well, really Daddy Mark's car because Doug doesn't have a car anymore—is already in front of my apartment. When Ryan knocks on my door, I tell him I am going to marry Doug. I don't even let him inside. At seventeen, I had decided that I needed to marry someone who believes in God and will go to church. Despite Ryan's priest training, or maybe because of it, Ryan doesn't have anything to do with church. Doug grew up in the same church as me, and that means he will follow the bible and take care of me, like a husband is supposed to take care of his wife. Somehow, I convince myself that my reasoning is sound, that Doug really will follow the bible. I am so tired that having someone take care of me is almost as important as having Tia grow up with her daddy. Tia needs her father. I am tired. Ryan and I still have to work together at the nursing home, but I know him well enough to know he will be respectful.

It's April Fools, so when Yasmin tells me she's in labor, at first, I think it's a joke. It's a one mile walk down Michigan Avenue to Butterworth Hospital, and there isn't a bus, so we have Junior stay with the babies, and Yasmin and I go together for the long walk. When we got there, the doctors took her into the room and stopped her labor. They say her petite body is rejecting the pregnancy because it has only been twenty months since she gave birth to Nadia at fourteen. After they treated her, Yasmin and I walked home. Over the course of the next few weeks, we walked back to the hospital five times with the same result. It's too early, but Yasmin's baby is determined to be born.

Once during the middle of the night, while we are walking back from the hospital, a guy comes out of a bar and follows us. As we near the light at Michigan and College, I see the guy is still there and I get scared. I tell Yasmin to run when I say run. I tell her she needs to get home as fast as she can. The thought creeps into my head: what if it's a green light, and we can't run? I don't want Yasmin to be scared, too, but I am not going to let anything happen to her. There aren't a lot of cars around, but there are still four blocks to go. We are walking as fast as we can because I don't want Yasmin to run any more than she has to, but the guy seems drunk and wobbly, and he's getting closer. I see the light has just changed to green for the same direction we are going so I know if we run, we'll make it across before the light changes. Then only one block to home. I cry out, "Run, run, this person is trying to get us."

I'm holding Yasmin's hand, and she squeezes tight as we run. Luckily, no cars are coming or even turning right on red, so we are able to sprint across the street and run walk the last block. I don't have my keys ready, but I hadn't locked the bottom door when we left, so I don't have to worry. We bolted into the door to the converted house where our apartment is, and I hurriedly locked the door from the inside. We are safe, though my heart is pounding, and I can't catch my breath for fear. Yasmin is panting, but she seems all right otherwise. When we get upstairs, I look out the front window and I can see the guy looking around, shaking his head. I sank to the couch in relief. We live in a pretty safe neighborhood, especially compared to my first apartment, but I hope we don't have to go out late at night again. When I'm married to Doug, he'll take care of us, and we won't have to worry about getting to places when we need to.

The sixth time's the charm. "Ms. Regina, we are going to let the baby be born today," the doctor spoke to me as her guardian. Yasmin is thirty-six weeks now and the baby should survive well even though it's a month to Yasmin's due date on June 15th. I'm so relieved--no more middle of the night walks to and from the hospital. Yasmin is the happy one as we hug because we are going to have a baby today. Her labor moves along fast. Yasmin's pain is intense, but I am there as before, letting her squeeze my hand. We are hoping for a boy, so we have already picked out a name. I insisted on the last name, Junior picked the first name, and Yasmin picked the middle name. When he is born, we welcome him. Jaymell Andre MOORE with joy. His last name will be Moore, not Carpenter, after our real daddy. His first name is after Daddy also, which Junior likes because he says he isn't a Junior anymore. Everyone called daddy Jay L, short for Jason Lee, but we made it Jaymell. So, the three of us named him the newest member of our family.

Two weeks after Jaymell was born, I finished my first year of college. Nobody can say I'm not a college student or that I won't make anything of my life like Daddy Mark said. I am glad I only took three classes this term because I had to increase my hours at work in the last few months to cover all our expenses. My report card wasn't as good as I wanted, and I ended up with two C's and one B. My grades don't show how hard I have been working to keep everything together or how tired I am. This is my third accounting class, Accounting III, and getting a C makes me question this double major. Since I went from an A to a B and finally a C in accounting, I decided I will have to drop the accounting part of my major. It will be okay, I tell myself. Besides, the computer 'thang' is going to take over the world. I believe that more now than I did when I started school. I am already learning COBOL and RPG programming languages, and I'm good at them. I'm going to be a Computer Programmer. When I finish, I'll get a job that will earn me more than my squashed dream of being a math teacher would have earned or even what a post office worker takes home. I'm going to do well in this life. I believe in me even if no one else does or even cares.

I met with Marianne again to register for my second and final year to earn my associates of science degree in Computer Programming. When I get to her office, she has my file out. She looks at my GPA that started at 3.43, then 3.04, and now at 2.90. I know what she is thinking, but I also know that she understands how much I have worked to get this far. She asks me in a voice full of kindness and concern, "Are you sure you want to continue college with the responsibilities you have?"

I tell her, "Yes, I'm getting married so my grades should go back up as I won't have to work so much." She looks at me with a face that says she is doubtful but still happy for me. I feel like she knows things about my life I couldn't even dream of much less imagine.

It's the summer of 1982, and I hope it will be as wonderful as our last few summers have been. This summer should be even better, though, because Doug and I are really getting married. My acceptance of his wry proposal was a hasty decision only two months ago. But we are going to be a normal family, just like the pastor said. I don't have college, so even with work I have free time to plan the wedding even though I don't know how to plan a wedding, and I only have $100 saved up. Doug doesn't have any money saved, and he's leaving it up to me. We're going to have this wedding without Daddy Mark and Mama Betty. We plan it for the week in July when they will be in Houston, and we all make sure they don't find out about it.

After Daddy Mark shot at me thinking that Doug was sleeping at my apartment, I assumed they would be against marriage. When I imagine Daddy Mark at my wedding, I picture him causing trouble and saying terrible things. I already know Daddy Mark is capable of extreme violence, and I'm still afraid of him. I'm also afraid they will stop Doug from coming to the wedding if they know about it, even though he is twenty-four. That would be a slap in the face. I am a little embarrassed about my relationship with Doug, so I'm not out telling everybody about our marriage anyway. I want Tia to have her father, so I won't let those other concerns overpower my desire to give her that gift.

When I call and tell my dad that I am getting married, he seems to be okay with me marrying Doug. My dad is even going to perform the ceremony now that he is an ordained minister. I need a maid of honor, and even though Rennie is my best friend, I decided to ask Taylor. She's the one who lived with me, and her mom said we can have the wedding in her backyard.

Before I knew it, Taylor and I went shopping for a dress at the mall. I tell her it can't be white since I have a three-year-old. We picked out a yellow flowered formal dress that hangs to the floor with a chiffon cape attached. It looks great on me even though it is a size nine and I wear a twelve. My big behind and boobs, plus the nine pounds I never lost from being pregnant, make me wear a size larger than Taylor and Rennie. That bothers me, always has, though Doug says I always had the best figure. I don't really believe him because he calls me knocked-kneed and says his dream girl is petite--but I want to. The dress cost $30, so I hope he likes it. I pray he does.

Now the cake and the honeymoon. The reception is going to have to be just cake and punch, sort of like the small weddings I have seen on tv. I ordered the cake from the place where I had gotten Tia's first cake. All I can afford is two layers, which is small, but enough, as not even a dozen people will be there. I purchase those prewritten packed invitations from the drugstore, and I write them out in my best handwriting. I invited Rennie, her mom, Taylor's mom, and a girlfriend from work, Laurie. Also, my dad and his wife got an invitation.

The honeymoon. Only $50 left, so I reserved a rental car for one day for $20 odd dollars, a fancy one to make it special, and the hotel on South Division is pretty new, so ok, right? It costs about $20 for a night. Dreaming of a big, beautiful wedding is not for me. I'm marrying my brother, adopted or not, and for a lot of people that will be a scandal. Making a big deal will attract attention. And I certainly don't want to do that.

A couple of weeks before the date, Doug and I headed down to the county clerk's office. The clerk looks at our completed application for the license and reads it out loud. She sees we have both put Mama Betty Withers as mother. "Siblings can't marry," she says. I say I am adopted, and my birth name is Regina Moore not Carpenter and Doug have his mother's maiden name of Withers instead of Carpenter like me because she wasn't married to Daddy Mark at the time. The clerk walks away from her desk for what seems like the longest twenty minutes ever. Maybe we can't marry. Then what am I going to do? Doug doesn't appear excited or disappointed or nervous like I am, but I think it is because he is confident. She returns shaking her head while saying it will be processed and to return in a week to pick it up. I sigh with relief. The wedding is on.

Before we can get married, I tell Doug two things: "I am not going to iron your shirts like your mother, and I am going to finish my education." He doesn't argue, so I think everything will be okay. I have been thinking I've been an adult for a while, but this feels like absolute proof. I am a grown woman.

Chapter 23

Trifecta

"I have learned that success is to be measured not so much by the position that one has reached in life as by the obstacles which [she] has had to overcome in order to succeed."
—Booker T. Washington

The day comes, and I feel beautiful in my dress. It is lovely, and I feel special thinking I am making up for the prom I couldn't go to. Rennie and Taylor always wear makeup, but I never have. It's one of the remnants of Mother Ackley's Pentecostal upbringing. Taylor puts eyeshadow and lipstick on for me. Now I have my hair and makeup just right, and even though it is hot, as I walk between the chairs we have set up in the backyard, I feel elegant. Tia is the flower girl, and she is adorable, but she doesn't really know what's happening. Rennie isn't here probably because Taylor is the maid of honor. Rennie has sent her younger brother to walk me down the aisle, which I go along with even though I don't really have a relationship with him. Doug doesn't have a best man, though Ryder was his best friend. But he couldn't invite him after what he did to him by getting me pregnant while I was supposed to be Ryder's girlfriend. They still talk some as far as I know. He was close to some of his cousins, but since we didn't want Daddy Mark and Mama Betty to find out, he couldn't tell any of them. Yasmin is there with Nadia and Jaymell. Junior isn't there, and I feel so heartbroken that I can't even talk about it.

Doug acts respectful to my daddy, and the ceremony is so fast that I hardly can remember it even a few minutes later. The only thing that stands out is my dad's lecture about how our marriage is supposed to be while we stand there sweating under the hot sun. He tells us that we must leave our families behind when we marry and put only each other first. I wonder if he is talking right to me, saying I should forget about Yasmin and Junior. This reminds me of how we were separated in our first foster homes, and I am miserable about it. Daddy does say something about leaving behind your mother and father, which is easy for me, but might be tricky for Doug since he is tied to his mother's apron strings, as the saying goes. This barely registers because I am thinking about why my daddy would want me to forsake Yasmin and Junior. Is that what's he's trying to say? I can't believe it. I keep thinking about how because of what I'm doing right now, Tia will have a mommy and daddy, a real family that no one can take away from her.

We have the cake and punch, and everybody seems pretty happy. We gather up our very few wedding gifts, and while my siblings and the kids go home, Doug and I get into the wedding rental car, and go to the hotel for our honeymoon. We are going to live in my apartment until we move into a rental home, but it feels special to have one night together as husband and wife. I wake up in the morning feeling like my new life is just about to begin.

I am nervous about telling Doug's parents, but when they get back, Mama Betty calls me all excited. The only thing that is important is Tia. Now that I am married to Doug, Mama Betty is acting like she has always been a loving mother to me. I think that somewhere deep down, I was hoping that if I married Doug, I would become blood, and she might love me. I am a mother now, having never really had one, so there is that gap in my life that I still hope somehow to fill.

Within three months, we moved into a little three-bedroom house at the end of a street in the hood. It's not too bad, and at least we can all fit. I make the dining room into a bedroom for Yasmin. I hear and sometimes see a boy sneaking in. One night, after seeing a boy leave, I tell her that she can't keep having boys over--there's no way I want her to get pregnant again. She shouts at me, and we are both angry, possibly for the first time ever. I don't want Tia and Nadia to see what is happening. But I can't help it and I say, "You are acting like a bitch!" Yasmin slaps me, hard. I'm not taking that--I have been hit enough to know you have to hit back. I slap Yasmin. We get into a fight and Doug comes and breaks us up. Yasmin says she isn't going to live with us anymore.

The social worker still visits every month, and I have to tell him that it's getting harder for me to keep Junior and Yasmin under control. Junior is going out with some wild kids, and Yasmin likes sneaking her boyfriend over.

They are old enough that they don't think they have to listen to me. The social worker have them become emancipated minors, and they go to live on Cass Street, in the worst part of town, because that is all the State can afford. I take food over to them whenever I can and hope they feel like they made the right tradeoff--they got their freedom but lost our family togetherness. Or maybe they just didn't want to live with me and Doug when we got married. I don't know for sure. So, I ended up being separated from Yasmin and Junior, just like my dad said, though I didn't want it to be that way.

I wanted to get custody of Nadia because she and Tia are so close, and it would be easier for Yasmin to just have the baby, who is so young he needs his mother. Yasmin says she'll think about it. However, Doug is very much against it. He says that Yasmin will probably come back to get Nadia when she gets older and that will be too hard for us. Nadia's grandmother wants her, too. She always has been good to Yasmin and Nadia, helping them out whenever she can. In the end, Yasmin keeps Nadia.

When I find out that I am pregnant, I am so excited. Everyone calls it the honeymoon baby. Since I was fourteen and Doug started paying attention to me, I had been infatuated with him, but something changed when we got married. Now, I think he loves me, and so I must love him. It's not the same as what I felt for Ryan, but I keep reminding myself that Doug is my husband now, and he's my babies' father. I had Doug go to probate court and establish paternity for Tia when she was one year old. Now I am going to have her name changed to Withers, Doug's last name, from Carpenter, the name I was forced to take when I got adopted. The name he had also, before we married. But it wasn't his legal name. Withers was. I have him added on Tia's birth certificate and they make a whole new one that looks like we were married when she was born. With the new baby I am having in wedlock, everything will be easier and wonderful. I'm still in college, but now I really have all the parts of life that I dreamed of, a father for my babies, a home, and hope for the future.

The joy doesn't last long. I miss my siblings. And it turns out that what I told Marianne was wrong. Life doesn't get easier after I get married. Doug is working part-time at Sears, so he can pay some of the bills. I still have to work while I'm in school. I'm sick from my pregnancy and taking care of patients--feeding them and changing their clothes and giving them baths--is hard work. I only have Tia at home now that Junior and Yasmin have their own place, so at least that is less work, but I still try to take them some groceries as much as I can. I'm learning to cook for Doug because I think that is what I'm supposed to do. Even though I told him I wasn't ironing his shirts and pants, I'm still the one who does all the cleaning around the house.

When fall comes, I take four classes at Davenport: Advance COBOL, College English II, Systems I, and Social Awareness. Just like I told Doug, I am still determined to finish school. I go to my boss and ask for four months off for school, but she says no. She won't hold my job for me. A white girl asks for time off to go on a study abroad trip, and she gets the time off with a job to come home to. I liked the girl, but I feel bad. Why is life so unfair? Why does she get time off for something fun in college while I can't get time off for college when I'm pregnant? I don't ask my boss or point out the difference, though. I do get to reduce my hours, which makes things a little better.

When the holidays come around, I'm excited because we're having Christmas as a family, just like on all the tv shows. We are in our own house, and I use my decorations to make it special. Doug gets a discount from Sears, so we get to go Christmas shopping there. We spoil Tia and buy gifts for Junior, Yasmin, Nadia, and Jaymell. The holidays are quiet and pleasant, but when my birthday comes around, I get my report card from Davenport, and I'm disappointed. My grades from the previous term are an A in COBOL and B's in English and Social Awareness. I got the first and only D in my life in Systems class. The sad thing is that I learned so much from that class. Everything in life is a system. I have no excuse or reason other than I just didn't have enough time or energy to do it all, so I take only three classes for spring trimester because I'm terrified of failing. For the next trimester, I enroll in Advanced RPG, Writing, and Principles of Basic.

I get better grades once I change to three classes, earning B's in my Advance RPG and in Principles of Basic, I tell myself again, that I made the right choice in this computer programming thing because I'm pretty good at it. I also got an A in Exposition Writing. My GPA is climbing back up.

We move to a better house because we want Tia to be in a safer neighborhood. Doug keeps working like he's a student instead of a family man. He even schedules his hours around *the game* on tv, and that means whatever game happens to be on. He loves sports, all sports, not just basketball and football, even golf. He knows the stats on every player and every team. I come home from school and work and sit next to him on my green couch, but he is so engrossed with the tv he barely notices me. He plays with Tia and has dinner with us, but otherwise he is either working, barely, or watching sports. I am going into my third trimester of my pregnancy and feel like I should get some special treatment, so I cut my hours back at work and expect Doug to pick up the slack. Instead, he gets his hours cut, so we don't have enough money to pay rent.

I am so angry. Doug says we have to move back with his parents, my parents too, I guess. We go to stay with Mama Betty and Daddy Mark. I'm so upset at Doug that I don't even have time to be afraid of Mama Betty and Daddy Mark. At least they play with Tia. I just go to class and come home to do my homework. We are only going to stay for a couple of months so we can save up a few paychecks, then we can get an apartment again before I have the baby. Every time I come home; Doug is in our bedroom sitting in front of the television watching sports. We sold all of the stuff we could, but we kept the tv and Tia's bed. He spends less hours at work than I spend just at school. One day, I came home with a lot of homework to do. Tia is downstairs with Mama Betty and Daddy Mark, and I don't know if Doug has seen her all day. He is sitting in front of the television watching basketball. I have a box of tools because I had to learn to fix things for myself. I open the box and pick up a hammer. I am thinking *that it is my tv, I brought it into the marriage, and Doug has no right to neglect his family for that tv*. It feels great as I lift my arm in the air for the first swing. I crash the hammer into the screen.

Doug yells, "What the hell?"

I swing the hammer into the screen again. The crash of glass brings Mama Betty upstairs.

"You don't pay attention to me or Tia. You just gotta watch the game. It's my tv, and you ain't gonna watch the game on my tv anymore." After that, we went for days without talking to each other. While I am at class, Doug takes the tv out to the trash. I had cleaned the glass out of the carpet. Doug tells me that his parents had pressured him to get me to marry him to avoid a statutory rape charge. Why didn't he tell me that in the first place? I don't let myself think about what that means. All he cares about is his mama, and I hate that. Anyway, Doug is embarrassed that we fought in front of his parents, and he finally comes up with enough money to get us an apartment. Did his parents help?

When we move, the apartment is nice and big. Tia gets her own room, and we have enough space in our bedroom for a crib. We don't have living room furniture yet, but I concentrate on making Tia's room nice and getting ready for the baby. The apartment is in a good area, and I try to convince myself that married life will be better here.

For the next trimester, I enroll in Business Applications, Business Law, and Math of Finance. They are going to be hard classes, but I feel good about Business Applications. I don't really know what it means, but it sounds interesting. The class I am most excited to take is Math of Finance since it has been a while since I dropped accounting as a major and I love math. Business Law is scary because everyone has told me how hard it is. But Business Law turns out to be one of my favorite classes. It's a requirement for everybody, so the instructor knows most of the students aren't going to be lawyers. I learn a lot legally…no pun intended. My instructor is a real lawyer who is so encouraging when I ask questions. He even says he wants to be my baby's godparent. He says it every time I stay after class to talk and even right during class. He has a good sense of humor and makes the class fun. I'm never sure if he really wants to be the godparent or if it's part of the fun of the class, but I think he admires my tenacity to stay in school. Having an instructor treat me in this friendly and positive way makes me feel comfortable about being pregnant as a student. It means a lot to me. Even though I have a big belly, I walk up and down the stairs and go to classes carrying my big stack of books.

My baby is due May 11 (the same day I had a miscarriage two years earlier), which means I will have her near the end of final trimester. I am so determined to finish my degree when I say I will that I won't let labor and delivery stop me. It's the first week of May and we go to the hospital excited and happy. Doug and I are hoping for a boy. He has picked out the name Mychal after his favorite basketball player *again*. When we are in the hospital, I say that we should think of a girl's name just in case. I want to have a name that will rhyme with Tia's because I think that will be cute and it will be a way to connect them.

It is a new trend in my culture to name kids' African names, and I think of the name Miasha, with Rennie for middle name, after my friend. While we are in the hospital room, Doug keeps falling asleep. Every time he snores, I call out to him, waking him up. It's upsetting that he isn't there for me. I thought he would be holding my hand and saying encouraging things. After only a couple of hours, the nurses took me into the delivery room. Doug stays in the hospital room. All the exercise and hard work I have had to do pay off because I have my baby in only four hours total. It's an easy delivery, and when the nurses take my new baby to clean her and take her to the nursery, I try to relax. I am so happy to have a little girl who is beautiful and wonderful and will be a playmate for Tia. The nurses wheeled me back to the room and brought her to me. As we are on the way, one of the nurses tells me she could hear Doug snoring down the hall while I was in labor. I am so embarrassed that my husband doesn't act like a regular husband, but I just laugh and say he is so tired. Maybe they will think he works really hard--they don't have to know.

When he sees our new baby girl, Doug is amazed at how tiny she is. He hadn't seen Tia right after she was born. Her nickname will be Mia. She was seven pounds eight ounces, exactly the average baby weight. Doug noticed how she had that odd hole in the top of her ears, just like him. It is a relief that he recognizes a sure sign that Mia is a Withers, knowing what his family feels about me. I stayed in the hospital the normal three days and then we all went back to our apartment. Kids can't come to the hospital, so I'm excited to get home to Tia and introduce her to her new sister. She loved her right away.

I had to contact all of my instructors to get my homework for the time I was out. When I am out of the hospital, I can take care of the new baby and Tia while I catch up on my homework, so I can graduate on time.

Just a few weeks later, at the end of the trimester, I earned all B's. I feel proud of myself for doing it even with the pregnancy and having a baby, plus the rest of life. I enrolled in the summer term to make up for only taking three credit hours for a few trimesters. I am still going to graduate on time with my Associate Degree of Science in Computer Programming. That sounds so good, and I keep repeating it to myself to stay motivated.

I take Macroeconomics, Office Machines and Poli Sci. Everyone said Macro Econ was hard for accounting people so it will be good to take it in summer when it's easier and instructors are more lenient. Students say the same about Poli Sci. But I love that class and what I get to learn about our government. (*Later in life, I become a self-proclaimed political pundit*). Office Machines is my favorite, and not because it is easy to me but because I learn how to use machines in an office setting. Learning how people in a real office use adding machines, calculators, copy machines, etc. makes me feel like I am close to being a professional person, too.

Needless to say, I ended my last term with all A's. I say it over and over again to myself, "All A's." I am so proud of myself. And I am graduating with a 3.07 GPA. Given all I have been though, that feels like a miracle. I have to remind myself that God must have been with me.

The same month, Yasmin graduates from her school, at just seventeen, even with two babies. Since I'd recently given birth, I was unable to attend her graduation. But, proud, nonetheless. Junior graduates from Ottawa Hills, the same school as me. He doesn't get to walk because he got into some trouble, but he is a high school graduate, and I feel proud that I passed on the importance of education to my siblings. Abandonment, foster care, adoption, abuse, none of that stopped any of us. We are all graduates of the class of **1983**.

One of the most exciting days of my life starts with my dad coming from Jackson. That is something really big because he hasn't come to visit since my wedding. He doesn't say it, but I know this shows how important it is and how proud of me he is. As I iron my graduation gown, I try to settle my nerves. I am wearing a comfortable dress and flats, just to be safe about walking across the stage--I don't want to trip and fall. I think about all of the teachers who have guided and encouraged me.

I know Mrs. Brown and Marianne will be proud of me. I have gotten my degree and will be a computer programmer. Just the thought sends shivers of excitement through my whole body. All of my tickets to the ceremony have been taken: my real daddy and his wife, Vanessa, Yasmin, and Doug are coming. Daddy Mark and Mama Betty stay home with Tia and Mia, who is only one month old. I can't believe that only a month ago, I was still pregnant and finishing college.

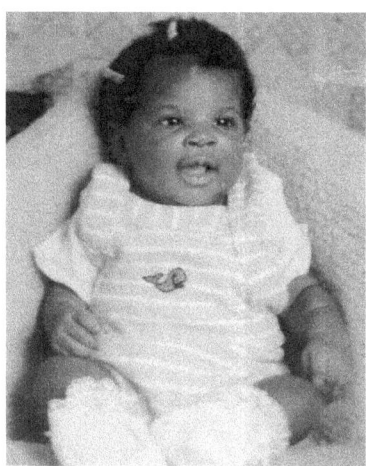 Mia 5 weeks

Like all the other graduates, I sit and listen to all of the speeches, not really paying attention to the words. I know because of my last name; I will be one of the last graduates called. I almost don't realize what is happening when my name is announced, "Regina Elissa Withers." I hear a loud whoop and recognize the voice. Even though the audience has been told not to yell out, Yasmin is cheering for me.

I walk carefully across the stage and shake the hand of the president of the college, Brenda Mieras, then turn to get my photo taken. I have the biggest smile ever because I want it to be the best picture I have ever taken. As I walk slowly off the stage, careful not to trip, Marianne stops me to give me a quick hug. I tear up as I feel her embrace, thinking I can't believe this is happening to me. When I get back to my seat, I exhale. Have I breathed at all during this whole ceremony? Joy is a funny thing. After the ceremony, I met my dad and Vanessa outside. He hugs me and says he is proud of me. Everybody congratulates me and I feel like everything in my life makes sense now. I am at the place I am supposed to be. I ask myself, "Am I okay, now? Just like Grandmo used to say? Is this the time I am worthy? Worthy of being loved?

My degree from Davenport comes in the mail in September 1983. Triumph and pride fill me to the point of almost exploding as I place it in the frame I'd been given when I walked the stage. I have done all this: sheltered my siblings and brought them to the brink of adulthood; had two beautiful daughters who I'd given a normal family with their real mom and real dad; overcome hunger, neglect, physical and sexual abuse, and fear; and walked a path for my siblings to follow. That is to graduate from college. Nothing stopped me from achieving my dream, not even ever seeing *her* again.

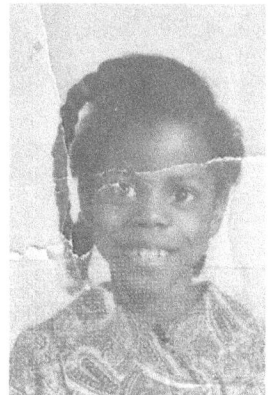 

age 5   *age 20*

All I wanted was to be able to independently take care of my family no matter what. I've done what I set out to do, got a college education to gain and maintain financial independence, helped my siblings through high school and placed hope in the next generation. School was my haven!

www.ingramcontent.com/pod-product-compliance
Lightning Source LLC
Chambersburg PA
CBHW071738120626
46550CB00002B/569